It's All About the Client

Consulting for Results

Doug Reeves gives practical and insightful advice to any business consultant. His primary focus is both unusual and refreshing in the typical consulting approach: Focus on the customer's business, not on the consultant's services. Only by understanding the customer, and the customer's business problems, can a consultant truly provide value. This concept is lost on most typical consultants, who seem focused on getting an engagement rather than understanding the customer.

—MARION K. JENKINS, PH.D.
CEO of QSE Technologies, Inc., and contributing author to *Business Driven Information Technology,* published by Stanford University Press

Great! The information in "The Needs Analysis: Pathology Report or Treasure Hunt?" is presented in a direct and coherent manner without all of the education fluff one usually reads. In my work with the Czech Republic as a consultant, I have since started changing behavior in working with my clients. Having read several books on this topic, I must say that this is the one that has captured it all and presented it in a format that is practical for use.

—THOM LOCKAMY
Chief Academic Officer, Norfolk Public Schools, Norfolk, Virginia

Doug Reeves's book is at once a framework, establishing and tying together the elements of the consultant's role, and a tough-minded set of guidelines for those intent on becoming highly effective. The book will prove highly useful to those early in their consulting careers, but it is much more than a primer; Reeves has staked out a comprehensive, challenging standard, against which many of us mid-career consultants will feel compelled to measure ourselves going forward.

—JEFFREY HOWARD, PH.D.
Founder, The Efficacy Institute, Waltham, Massachusetts

Doug Reeves's message in It's All About the Client *is the most intellectually accurate and stimulating, emotionally honest and intelligent, career-inspiring and -enhancing, and client-friendly exposé that I have ever read or heard about on the subject of consulting.*

—DUKE NIELSEN
Human Resources Management consultant

Accountability for Learning: How Teachers and School Leaders Can Take Charge

Accountability in Action: A Blueprint for Learning Organizations, Second Edition

Assessing Educational Leaders: Evaluating Performance for Improved Individual and Organizational Results

Crusade in the Classroom: How George W. Bush's Education Reforms Will Affect Your Children, Our Schools

Holistic Accountability: Serving Students, Schools, and Community

Making Standards Work: Implementing Standards-Based Assessments in the Classroom, School, and District, Third Edition

On Common Ground: The Power of Professional Learning Communities

101 More Questions & Answers about Standards, Assessment, and Accountability

101 Questions & Answers about Standards, Assessment, and Accountability

Reason to Write: Help Your Child Succeed in School and in Life Through Better Reasoning and Clear Communication

Reason to Write: Student Handbook, Elementary Edition

The Daily Disciplines of Leadership: How to Improve Student Achievement, Staff Motivation, and Personal Organization

The Leader's Guide to Standards: A Blueprint for Educational Equity and Excellence

20-Minute Learning Connection: A Practical Guide for Parents Who Want to Help Their Children Succeed in Schools (Six state Editions)

For a listing of current articles in periodicals, please visit www.MakingStandardsWork.com/Resources.

It's All About the Client

Consulting for Results

Douglas B. Reeves

A L P
**Advanced
Learning
Press**

Advanced Learning Press

317 Inverness Way South, Suite 150

Englewood, CO 80112

Phone (800) 844-6599 or (303) 504-9312 ∎ Fax (303) 504-9417

www.AdvancedLearningPress.com

Editor: Graves Editorial Services

Design and Production: Graphic Advantage, Ltd.

Library of Congress Cataloging-in-Publication Data:

Reeves, Douglas B.; 1953–

    It's all about the client : consulting for results / Douglas B. Reeves.

       p.   cm.

  Includes bibliographical references and index.

    ISBN 0-9644955-6-2 (pbk.)

    1. Business consultants—Handbooks, manuals, etc.   2. Consultants—Handbooks, manuals, etc.   3. Success in business—Handbooks, manuals, etc.   4. Consulting firms—Management—Handbooks, manuals, etc.   5. New business enterprises—Management—Handbooks, manuals, etc.   I. Title

  HD69.C6R425 2005

  650.1—dc22   2005045371

Printed in the United States of America

10 09 08 07 06 05   01 02 03 04 05 06 07 08 09

To Julia

Acknowledgments

Cathy Shulkin reviewed every word of the text and, remarkably, did so while maintaining my quarter-million-mile travel schedule and every detail of more than 100 client engagements each year. She is intelligent enough to ask naïve questions and supportive enough to be demanding of my best work. She is sufficiently confident to risk confrontation rather than let quality lapse; and she shares a focus on quality that allows me to bear the role of consultant with pride and confidence.

Anne Fenske was the fairy godmother who launched this project, encouraging me to expand it from a single presentation into a book-length manuscript. I have witnessed Anne's intellectual growth from exceptional graduate study to corporate leadership to entrepreneurial excellence at Advanced Learning Press. She single-handedly quintupled the product lines for this venture and created a profound increase in the value of this organization. If you want a lesson about the leverage that a career in consulting can provide, then invest in a couple of cups of decaf coffee and Anne might share some of her insights with you.

My colleagues at the Advanced Learning Centers are an exceptional lot. They have displayed the power of ideas over personality. Though they are willing to challenge me in many respects, they have proven me right in at least one: There is a reason that this organization does not have my name in it. Ideas, not personalities, prevail over time. In particular, I wish to acknowledge the intellectual and personal contributions of Greg Atkins, Laura Besser, Ken Bingenheimer, Cheryl Bonnell, Sherry Burcham, Jan Christinson, Mia Dellanini, Sarah Denker, Cheryl Dunkle, Tony Flach, Todd Gilmore, Robin Hoey, Liz Hunt, Mary Kate Karr-Petras, Michelle LePatner, Matt Minney, Peggy Morales, Jason Mueller, David Nagel, Angela Peery, Peg Portscheller, Stacy Scott, Raymond Smith, Jill Unzicker-Lewis, David Scarbeary, Cindy Wasinger, Stephen White, Mike White, Amy Whited, and Nan Woodson.

I am particularly indebted to Larry Ainsworth, Executive Director; Eileen Allison, Professional Development Associate; Lisa Almeida, Professional Development Associate; Nan Caldwell, Senior Director of Client Relations; and Donna Davis, Senior Director of Professional Development, for their contributions to Chapter 11 and continued devotion to their clients and the field of consulting.

Three people in particular are responsible for transforming my dream of a consulting enterprise into reality. Andrew Reeves—entrepreneur, philanthropist, Little League coach, and terrific brother—provided the capital that allowed our company to move from a kitchen table to a city office. His wise counsel and essential confrontations have guided our multimillion-dollar growth. J.B. and Julie Reeves provided encouragement, resources, and unconditional love during the early and turbulent days of this enterprise. It is too late to thank my father in these pages, but not too late to embarrass my mother, about whom you will read much more in the pages that follow. Whether you approach the challenges of the consulting life in your eighteenth or eightieth year, these people will provide inspiration and practical advice.

Julia, to whom this book is dedicated, is a good person. I struggle mightily with what I could say about a 16-year-old daughter whom I adore and who is an unending source of pride for her mother and me. She is passionate about friends, animals, school, and principles. She is angry about the right things and tolerant of things that do not matter. She is the world's best older sister and younger sister, sandwiched between two brothers who do not go out of their way to make her life easier. Yet she never misses an opportunity to tell her brothers that she loves them. She is a patient and endearing granddaughter, spending time with Nonnie and Papa when her cohorts might find the wisdom of the ages too boring for consideration. Thus, to call her a "good person" may seem faint praise, but it is in fact my highest accolade. I hope that the same will be said of me some day.

About the Author

Douglas B. Reeves, Ph.D.

Dr. Douglas Reeves is an internationally recognized consultant in leadership and learning, having worked on five continents and all 50 of the United States. He is the author of 19 books, and his articles have appeared in national and international journals and newspapers throughout the world; his work has been translated into Chinese, Spanish, and Hebrew. Twice named to the Harvard University Distinguished Authors Series, Dr. Reeves delivers more than 50 keynote addresses to education, government, nonprofit, and business audiences each year. He lives near Boston and can be reached at dreeves@ LeadAndLearn.com.

Contents

CHAPTER 11

Introduction

So, you want to be a consultant? Despite all the cartoons, jokes, and cynicism directed our way, let me be the first to welcome you to an honorable profession. We are teachers, communicators, problem solvers, and most importantly, responsible for empowering people and organizations to reach higher levels of performance and satisfaction. We can accept quite a few comic jabs aimed our way—I'll even share a few in these pages—if we can wake up every day with the confidence that our work has meaning and purpose. In the following pages, you will hone that meaning and purpose to a sharp edge, defining yourself and your services. You will learn the professional methods that have been successful for our clients and my organization, Advanced Learning Centers, and you will also learn the business methods that have helped make the consulting enterprise successful.

Whether your clients will be large or small businesses, nonprofit organizations, governmental organizations, or individual consumers, these ideas will help you improve your service, communication, and marketing. This book is not just about your clients; it's about you and your partners and employees. Great consulting organizations not only meet the needs of their clients, they also help their employees buy homes and cars, pay college tuition for themselves and their children, support their communities and charitable organizations, and provide a secure retirement and financial independence for their families. The lessons contained in these pages are based on what is arguably one of the most successful consulting firms in the country, whether success is measured in client satisfaction, client repeat business, or financial growth.

You will also learn from my mistakes, and I will not spare the confessions, however embarrassing they may be. We have worked in all 50 states and on five continents. I have personally traveled more than two million miles in the past ten years. I wish I could claim that every engagement was flawless, every planning session perfect, and every quality rating a solid 10. But I can't, and the unvarnished truth about my personal and organizational mistakes will help you as much as my successes.

One of my many quirks is that I almost always read backward. If I'm reading an academic article, I read the references to get an idea of the intellectual history of the article. If I'm reading a magazine, I read from back to front so I'll be sure to catch the articles I might have missed had I been seduced by the catchphrases of the cover or table of contents. When I read a book, I look at the appendices—the pages most people disregard entirely. Just in case you are a similarly nonlinear person, let me offer a preview of what lies ahead, and then you can choose to explore this volume in the way that suits you best. At the end of this book, you will be given practical tools that you can use to develop a new consulting enterprise or to expand and improve the consulting organization you already have. These tools are yours. You will find interview forms, sample contracts, checklists, and other tools that I have found useful. You can copy the appendices, modify them, or use them however you choose. If you copy them, we ask only that you continue to use our copyright notice on each form.

Chapter 1 introduces you to client relationships, and suggests that the first lesson for every consultant is that it is not about us, but about the client. *The client's needs are paramount.* Moreover, we must not only explore their needs, but we must also identify and reinforce their strengths. When consultants focus exclusively on problem solving, they fail to recognize, respect, and leverage the strengths that the client has. If our ultimate goal is—as it must be—the creation of new and improved client capacity, then we must learn the cardinal rule of organizational leadership: It is faster and easier to build on strengths than to compensate for weaknesses.

Chapter 2 suggests that consultants must know themselves better than they know a client. We know not only who we are but also, of equal importance, who we are not. Every consultant and consulting organization is defined by the engagements it declines. If the qualifications for a prospective client consist only of a normal body temperature and full bank account, the consultant is doomed to failure. Making demands on a client might strike some readers as emblematic of the prima donna ("I *must* have Perrier, not tap water!"). Indeed, I have had clients tell me about a consultant who waited at an airport while complaining that the limousine the client sent to pick him up was not long enough. Suffice to say that that particular consultant has disappeared from the scene, and is now more likely to be driving a limo than riding in one.

Some demands, though, are appropriate; indeed, essential. If your job is to communicate with your client's employees, then you must demand—that is not too strong a word—that the employees be in an environment that is conducive to adult learning. If your job is to coordinate policy, planning, and implementation of a complex project, then you must demand that the leadership in key areas be present at the table. When W. Edwards Deming, the greatest quality consultant of the twentieth century, undertook an engagement, he did not begin until the client's chief executive officer was present; if that key leader departed the meeting, Dr. Deming would politely assemble his materials and leave the room as well.

Chapter 3 addresses the delicate issue of marketing. After all, this is not coffee, toilet tissue, or soap—it's *you*. But wait: Surely sales and marketing are beneath contempt as tools for professional services? Although I have built a multimillion-dollar organization without spending a dime on advertising in the past eight years, I would not downplay the importance of sales and marketing. Marketing is all about learning what clients need, and sales is all about connecting the capabilities of a vendor with the needs of a client. Every organization needs these essential skills, and great consultants model those skills in their relationships with clients.

Chapter 4 addresses the issue of passion, the subject of one in an endless series of consultant jokes. Nevertheless, *passion* is not too strong a word to describe the intensity of feeling for what we must do. This is an enterprise of relationships, and relationships invariably involve emotions. Although I do not love every client, I must love what I do. I must love what I create for those clients. I must love what our mutual work can do for the client and for my organization. I must equally hate the alternative. It becomes a moral and ethical issue: We are right and the alternative is wrong. This work is too hard for ambivalence to prevail. You must be passionate about the cause, the method, and the result.

Chapter 5 addresses the business end of consulting. I have learned these lessons the hard way, and the revelation of my mistakes will save you many times the price of this book. You will be tempted to offer discounts, only to find out that your discount was used to pay for the services of your arch-competitor. You will be tempted to offer credit, only to discover that the credit terms offered by other vendors followed the Leo Durocher rule that "nice guys finish last." If you have disagreements—and any large and successful business is likely to have some—you will learn ways to deal with them.

Chapter 6 addresses the logistical elements of consulting, including travel and technology. In more than 12 years of doing this work, I have missed only one engagement. I have driven all night, chartered private airplanes, taken all-night busses, had $200 cab rides, and done everything short of hitchhiking (so far) to meet a client's needs, but I have missed only the one (because of a snowstorm). The other side of that dreary picture is that I make a point of treating my colleagues exceptionally well. Because our first priority is giving clients our very best efforts, we make profligate use of airline and hotel upgrades and give special treatment to our "Century Club" members who spend more than 100 nights on the road. Whether you have an organization of one person or one hundred, it is essential that you treat yourself well when traveling, so that you can always give your clients your very best.

Chapter 7 addresses the issue that every consultant must eventually face: whether to go it alone or to build an organization. Cartoonist Scott Adams, of "Dilbert" fame, has deliberately avoided having employees, perhaps because he wishes never to become the pointy-haired boss that he ridicules in his popular and entertaining comic strip. Many successful consultants have done the same, writing their own invoices, collecting their own bills, and operating independently. Others have decided to build an organization. I will do my best to present both alternatives fairly.

Chapter 8 is a tough one, dealing with quality. In my organization, we evaluate quality as does our local Ira Motor Group, one of the largest and most successful auto dealership networks in the world. It doesn't make any difference if you have a major overhaul or an oil change, if you bought a $70,000 Lexus or a $15,000 used car. Every customer transaction is evaluated for quality, and if the quality is not exceptional, there is an immediate reaction. In my organization, I personally call the client if there is anything less than a 7 on our 10-point quality scale. Twice in the past 12 years and almost 10,000 engagement days, we have instituted the "wax your car and wash your dog" response. That means that if the quality of our service was not satisfactory, I personally call and ask the client, "How about if we give you all your money back, plus additional free service that I will personally deliver, AND wax your car, and wash your dog—would that make it okay?" Even when a client has been so upset that she could spit, this is usually good for a smile, and in every single case so far, it has transformed an unhappy client into an intensely loyal client who talks about our commitment to quality and performance to anyone who will listen. I don't like to work for free, and washing dogs and waxing cars is not my cup of tea either. But this exceptionally high quality standard sets us apart from other consulting firms, and if we received a low quality rating, I would be on an airplane tomorrow, carrying my car wax and dog brush.

Chapter 9 addresses business organizational issues. Things such as bonus plans, 401(k) plans, and employee stock ownership plans may seem remote to you now, but these have been the value drivers for our organization. My personal goal in the next few years is to make ten of my colleagues millionaires. It's not Microsoft or any of the high-tech stories of the 1990s, but it's a fair and reasonable goal considering the value we have created and the fair and just way in which we share that value with our most productive employees.

Chapter 10 addresses life and work, the most delicate of balances. Every day I go to work, every time I get on an airplane, and every time I meet with a client, I must ask and answer this question: If it all falls apart tomorrow, could I go back to teaching middle school math? Could I go back to mowing lawns? Could

I go back to selling shoes in a mall? Could I do those tasks that other people reject as menial and, from those beginnings, rebuild an organization and a life? If the answer is in the affirmative, then I can continue to take risks, serve clients, and build an organization. The day the answer to any of those questions is negative, my entrepreneurial days are over. When someone is chained to a mortgage, lifestyle, or personal identity that does not allow failure, they will invariably prefer safety, security, and the path of least resistance over challenge, innovation, and entrepreneurship. I know that life could crumble around me and I could start over, and still have those things in my life that matter most. That is what defines me as a person and the creator of an organization. Your life as a consultant will entail risk and creativity. On your most successful engagements, you will be tempted to rejoin the world of salaried employees, seeking tenure and a pension. If that is your heart's desire, you have my best wishes. But if you seek not only contentment and security, but also challenge and risk, opportunity and reward, and most of all the ability to choose your own destiny, then the consulting profession is for you.

Chapter 11 represents a synthesis of views from my colleagues, veteran consultants who offered their replies to the question, "What do you know now that you wish you had known when you started consulting?" This advice is straight from the journals of a few of our most successful and prolific consultants. Their advice, ranging from client relationships to the vagaries of travel, conclude this book on a practical note that will keep you firmly grounded in the reality that clients expect and that you will need as you embark on this exciting career.

April 2005   DOUGLAS B. REEVES
                                                                Swampscott, Massachusetts

Needs: Connecting with Your Client

The Needs Analysis: Pathology Report or Treasure Hunt?

Results

Defining Client Expectations

Morale, Relationships, and Emotional Intelligence

The Real Client

Client-Centered Engagements

Here are the five most important words in your consulting career: *It's all about the client*. It's not about how smart you are, how capable you are, where you went to school, or what stellar successes you have had in the past. It's not about your presentation abilities, facilitation skills, organizational prowess, or analytical insight. *It's all about the client.*

Remember the "wax your car and wash your dog" standard from the introduction? That's where I personally agree to wax the car and wash the dog of an unsatisfied client. On those very rare occasions (approximately .02 percent of our total engagements) when I have had to make good on that promise, the cause was a consultant who thought that the focus of the engagement was the consultant's background and experience rather than the client's need. Tattoo it on your forehead in reverse so that you will read it in the mirror: *It's all about the client.*

In this chapter, we will explore how to conduct a meaningful needs analysis so that you maintain the focus of your engagement where it belongs: on the needs of the client. The needs analysis must be supplemented by careful pre-engagement conferences that consider every detail of on-site engagements. We then turn our attention to results, as defined by the client, and propose the Results Paradox, a warning to consultants who believe that an exclusive focus on results is in the best interest of the client. Finally, the chapter considers the contrast between client-centered engagements and consultant-centered engagements. Although a healthy ego is clearly essential for consulting success, the most effective consultants place the client's needs, not the consultant's prowess, at the center of every engagement.

The Needs Analysis: Pathology Report or Treasure Hunt?

Consider your first seconds of client contact. Perhaps they responded to your letter or advertisement. Maybe they took your call or had a referral from one of your satisfied clients. Conceivably you were lucky enough to sit next to them on a cross-country flight and had a captive audience. But whether the context is a 6-hour flight, a formal meeting, or a 120-second elevator ride, you have only a few seconds to engage the interest of this prospective client. During these moments, the clients will decide if you are meeting your needs or their needs. The clients will decide if you are the purveyor of one more short-term diversion or if you are capable of solving their practical business problems. The clients will decide, in brief, if they should be interested in you because, above all, *you are interested in them.*

Let's assume that you cross this first hurdle, which puts you about 90 percent ahead of your competition. The 90 percent you left in the dust are those with canned solutions to problems that may or may not exist. They assumed that whatever they were selling was what the client needed. They were talkers, not listeners. They have a string of one-shot engagements by clients who were fooled once by bluster, but they never have the long-term relationships that create the careers of successful consultants. Having successfully surpassed 90 percent of your competition, you must now determine how to get past the remaining 10 percent so that you are in the top 1 percent of people who call themselves consultants and actually make a living at it.

Now that you have positioned yourself as a problem solver, genuinely interested in clients and their needs, the great temptation is to focus only on the needs, challenges, and weaknesses of the client—but not on the client's strengths. You have the client's attention, because you are genuinely interested in her and you want to solve her problems, but you must be equally diligent in discovering the fundamental strengths of this client. While the person engaging the consultant may see only organizational weaknesses that must be remedied, there are many other people in the organization who see in every remedy a threat to their professional and personal survival. These threats trigger their instinctive "fight or flight" mechanism; the organizational battlefield is littered with the remains of consultants who ignored the power of deep institutional resistance to change.

Many people assume that consultants are summoned by organizations to solve problems and address challenges that the organization cannot solve by itself. This misperception lies at the heart of the conflict that frequently emerges between a consultant and the client. Where one person in the client organization sees a problem requiring a solution, that person's colleagues see blame, accusation, and encroachment on personal and organizational territory. The consultant who satisfies the first person without meeting the needs of the entire organization will meet the fate of Achilles, who was brave in battle and resilient in the face of defeat, but ultimately was blinded by his personal ambition. The famous wound to his heel, inflicted by a far lesser combatant, caused his downfall. What is the Achilles' heel of the consultant? It is an exclusive focus on the personal preferences of a single individual within the organization and failure to consider the needs of the entire organization.

The fundamental need of any organization and the people within it is survival. Organizational theorists more fond of slick quotations than understanding will misquote Charles Darwin to claim that "survival of the fittest" is the primary rule of evolutionary biology and the law of the organizational jungle. In fact, Darwin theorized, with considerably greater nuance, that survival depends not on elimination of the slow and weak, but on successful adaptation to the environment. Although adaptation may, in part, depend on the elimination of weaknesses, it depends far more on the recognition, application, and development of strengths.

Every organization, no matter how dysfunctional, has strengths. A cardinal principle of leadership is that it is faster and easier to build on strengths than to compensate for weaknesses (Buckingham & Clifton, 2001). The challenge faced by every consultant is how to reconcile the strengths of an organization with the weaknesses that caused the organization to need your services in the first place. The best way to deal with this dilemma is the *needs analysis* (a sample is shown in Appendix A). Getting the needs analysis questionnaire completed will require persistence verging on relentlessness, because a successful needs analysis requires a greater degree of tenacity than most consultants possess and more cooperation than most impatient clients will provide. "Look—we just want these services and we don't have time to give you our strategic plan and organizational chart, and you certainly can't have 30 minutes of our CEO's time for an interview," they might protest. But if you are going to do anything—from Web site design to customer service training to leadership development to any other meaningful consulting work—for an organization, whether of two people or 200,000, you must take the time to conduct a needs analysis, with particular emphasis on the previous successes as well as current challenges.

Organizations that are seeking outside help sometimes do not believe in their own success. When you ask, "How did this department improve quality so much in the third quarter last year?" or "Why did shipping improve its efficiency so dramatically in July?" or "What caused Web site orders to spike on Tuesdays?" or "Why was employee satisfaction so high two years ago?," the responses will likely be, "We didn't know we had done any of those things well. We were so focused on how messed up we were, we didn't know we did anything right." When clients are fixated on mistakes, they are blind to the successes that are their core strengths. When a consultant fails to recognize those successes, the organizational energy that might have been channeled into making the consulting initiative a success will instead be directed against it, like an organism fighting invasion by a foreign substance. Successful consultants are the allies of the organism, not the invader, because they know that results will be achieved only by a coherent effort by the entire organization.

Results

What does the client mean by the word *results* anyway? In the business context, it might mean revenues, profits, customer satisfaction, employee engagement, quality, public perception, or any number of quantitative indicators. In the nonprofit sector, results might range from donations to continuous grant support to audience approval to client satisfaction. Every sector, from medical care to the military, from personal services to manufacturing, from child care to law firms, measures results differently. A consistent feature of a focus on results, however, is that the focus is simultaneously too broad and too narrow. It is the Results Paradox: The more myopic the focus on results, the lower the probability that the results will improve. An important

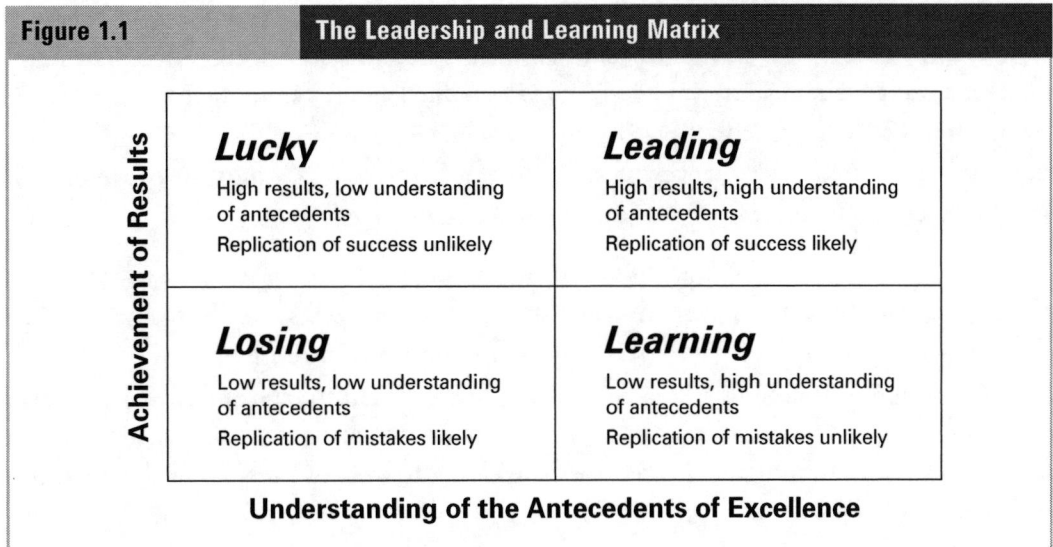

Figure 1.1   **The Leadership and Learning Matrix**

Achievement of Results

Lucky
High results, low understanding
of antecedents

Replication of success unlikely

Leading
High results, high understanding
of antecedents

Replication of success likely

Losing
Low results, low understanding
of antecedents

Replication of mistakes likely

Learning
Low results, high understanding
of antecedents

Replication of mistakes unlikely

Understanding of the Antecedents of Excellence

corollary is this: A myopic focus on process rather than results yields neither improved results nor improved processes. Only a comprehensive focus, as Figure 1.1 indicates, leads an organization to achieve an optimal, multifaceted view of both results and the antecedents of excellence.

Figure 1.1 illustrates the necessity of a more complex set of considerations than a single-minded focus on results alone. The vertical axis displays the classic focus on results, typically expressed in quantitative terms. "I don't care how you get there, just show me the results!" exclaims the impatient chief executive. Unfortunately, as Enron so dramatically illustrated, it is possible to satisfy the insatiable with short-term results while sacrificing the long-term survival of the enterprise. In 1999, Enron was honored in *Fortune* magazine as "America's Most Innovative Company," and was ranked "No. 1 in Quality of Management" and "No. 2 in Employee Talent" of all American companies. The magazine also acknowledged Enron as one of the 25 best places to work in America (Enron, 2000). Enron's innovative practices were widely heralded, used as case studies at the Harvard Business School, and appeared to be a solid basis for its ever-rising stock price. In other words, the results themselves appeared to justify the results. By such logic, trees grow to the sky. After all, the trees are higher this year than last year, and higher last year than the year before. It must continue that way forever. Alas, trees, like Enron, come crashing down if the presumption of uninterrupted growth is allowed to go unchallenged.

A myopic focus on results can lead to ignoring other important considerations. Furthermore, results themselves can be internally inconsistent and even counterproductive. For example, an exclusive focus on revenue growth without a consideration of profitability could allow a company to sell itself right out of business. One of the fastest ways to fuel revenue growth is heavy discounting. Such a strategy, however, adds little to shareholder equity if revenue growth is pursued at the expense of profitability. Conversely, if profits are the sole consideration, an easy way to raise profits is to cut costs. However, if cost cutting leads to a diminution of quality or employee engagement, any profitability will be short-lived.

In education, the current craze is to raise test scores. However, the fastest way for any high school in America to raise test scores is to increase the dropout rate among its lowest-performing students when the high-stakes tests are administered. Although such a strategy may make the numbers look good, it offers little in the way of social value, and creates a great deal in the way of long-term social and personal costs. In medical care, the fastest way to improve results, if the measurement of results is a zero death rate, is never to take a surgical risk with a patient. Never mind that such a strategy would allow a patient to die a slow, painful death from congestive heart failure; at least the death would not be associated with the surgical procedure on the operating table. In sum, the pursuit of results is a complex endeavor, and a myopic focus on results will inevitably lead to the Results Paradox in which the focus on results undermines results.

The matrix in Figure 1.1 offers two dimensions, including a consideration of the complexities of results on the vertical axis and a consideration of the antecedents of excellence on the horizontal axis. As the upper left-hand quadrant suggests, if an organization achieves high results, but does not understand how it achieves them, that organization is not good, but merely lucky. Consider the nonprofit organization that receives an anonymous donation of $1 million, sufficient to sustain its operating budget for a full year. Although such a windfall may allow the board of trustees to slap itself on the back for prudent financial management and superior fund-raising skills, such conclusions would be not only unwarranted, but also dangerous to organizational health.

Because the organization is unable to determine how the gift was procured, where it came from, or when it was given, it is very unlikely that such a gift can be replicated. In fact, the converse is true. An organization that achieves financial stability in the short term, without understanding why, will become complacent, depending on mystery and good fortune rather than prudence and diligence. The dot-com bubble of the 1990s was populated by companies in the "Lucky" quadrant; they were persuaded that rising stock prices reflected the genius of their founders rather than a transient association between the existence of the company, its popular labeling, and the madness of crowds. Just as favorable winds make the amateur sailor appear more expert, so rising markets make brilliant strategists of us all.

Sometimes unfavorable conditions also allow a leader to conflate effectiveness with luck. During times of recession, leaders are able to attract talent and maintain good workers, even though leaders fail to offer engaging workplaces, stimulating work environments, financial security, or meaningful work (perhaps the most important variable of all for long-term employee engagement). Thus, during a recession, leaders can brag about their low turnover rates and apparent high employee morale and satisfaction. Nevertheless, just as the dynamism of markets bursts every bubble, the resilience of the economy confounds every leader who believes that swagger and bullying are effective leadership tactics. In all these cases, short-term effectiveness was merely luck, and luck—as every casino owner knows—never lasts.

In the lower left-hand quadrant are the Losers, enterprises that not only show perpetually low results, but also remain perpetually clueless about their performance. The premise of the movie *The Eternal Sunshine of the Spotless Mind* (the title is a line from a poem by Alexander Pope, 1688–1744) is the existence of a brain manipulation procedure that selectively eliminates memories that are too painful for people to possess. Business is particularly brisk around Valentine's Day, as jilted lovers seek to obliterate any memory of their former heartthrobs. Any leader can have a bad day, quarter, or year (and every leader does), but it takes dogged persistence and the proverbial "spotless mind" to maintain the breathtakingly belligerent indifference displayed by some leaders. For example, one leader obliterated billions of dollars in shareholder value, taking a mutual fund from $3 billion to $185 million in a matter of five years (Einhorn, 2004). It is not difficult to think of examples from multiple sectors where indifference to poor results and similar indifference to causes combined to create disaster. This phenomenon extends from Napoleon at Waterloo, to the United States in Vietnam, to physicians in the nineteenth century who left their hands unwashed because they refused to accept the suggestions of the lowly midwives who suspected that rampant maternal and infant death might be associated with the practices of the doctors who delivered babies. Some parents in the twenty-first century refuse to give their children life-saving vaccinations and other medical treatments because neither medical evidence nor the death of children they love is greater than their need to be consistent in their philosophies.

The Leadership and Learning Matrix suggests not a destination, but rather the use of two continua, as displayed in Figure 1.2. The left-hand side of the matrix can best be referred to as the *victim continuum,* in which organizations and individuals haplessly bound from lucky to losing with neither direction nor clarity. The opportunities for any consultant to be effective on this side of the matrix are nil. Indeed, the consultant's fundamental obligation is not simply to "get results," but rather to move the organization and the individuals within it from the left side of the matrix

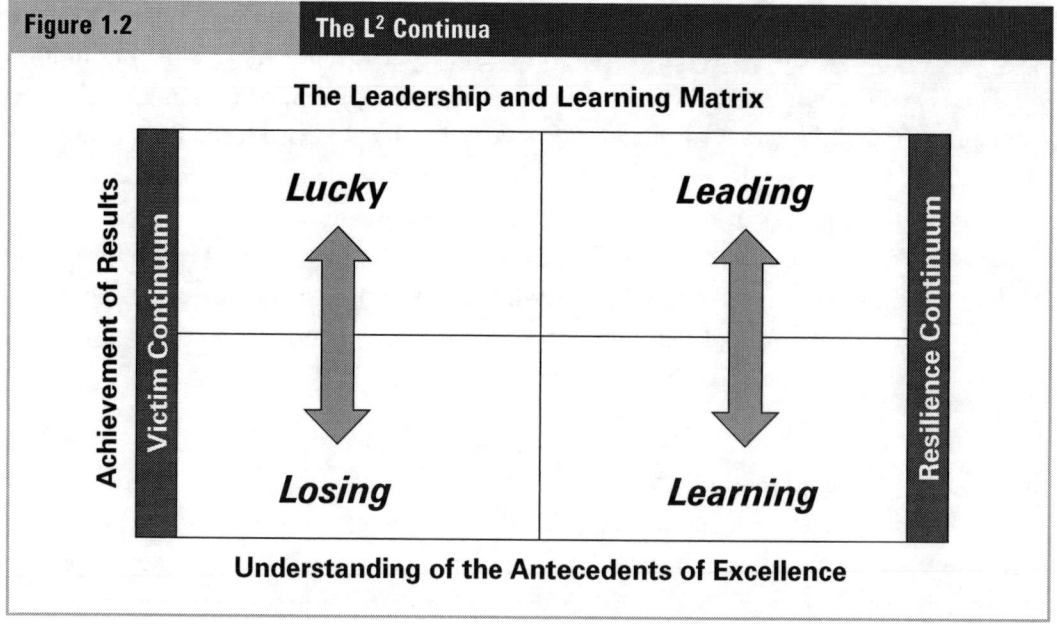

Figure 1.2 — The L² Continua

The Leadership and Learning Matrix

to the right, from the victim continuum to the resilience continuum. Operating at their peak, consultants provide organizational resilience, giving their clients the capacity to move from learning to leadership, from low results with deep understanding to high results and the accompanying understanding that will improve the likelihood that those high results can be replicated.

In the lower left-hand quadrant, consultants will enter an organization and step over the remains of many other consultants, programs, and interventions, all of which were briefly considered, tried without enthusiasm or deep implementation, and ultimately were discarded because, after all, they didn't work. Because clients in the losing quadrant frequently have rapid turnover in the executive suite, there remains substantial opportunity for quick-buck artists who seek the consulting equivalent of a one-night stand, eager to take the money and run, knowing that the likelihood of long-term impact is minimal. Fortunately, long-term consulting relationships are built on the right side of the matrix, not the left. You will be defined many times in your career by the engagements you decline—and declining to work with either the lucky or the losing will be one of the most important decisions any consultant can make.

The ideal client is in the lower right-hand side of the matrix. The results are low and the client understands that they are low. Moreover, the client has an appreciation that results alone are not a sufficient focus. The client understands that just as results are complex, so are the antecedents of excellence. There may be instances in which the client demonstrates an extraordinary strength, depth, and ability, yet none of those strengths are apparent in an environment in which low results cast a pall over every conversation. Among the most critical contributions that great consultants can make are the identification and definition of the antecedents of excellence.

These are never quick fixes, and they can be associated with variables whose relationship to results is not always immediately obvious. The Gallup Organization (Buckingham & Clifton, 2001) has brilliantly illustrated the relationship between nonobvious antecedents and organizational results. For example, organizations in which employees are able to agree with the statement, "I have a best friend at work," or "I get a chance to do what I do best almost every day," tend to have lower turnover, higher growth, and higher profitability than comparable organizations in which employees do not share these views. Although this research is based on extensive studies of thousands of organizations and more than 1 million employees, the research is perpetually greeted by skeptics who simply do not believe it. Other Gallup research suggests that effective leaders should not treat all employees equally, but rather should take a deliberately differentiated approach to everything from training to promotion to discipline. Although this is not what classical leadership training teaches, particularly in an environment fraught with litigation and committed to the appearance of fairness through cookie-cutter leadership techniques, the evidence is undeniable. *Differentiated leadership works.*

Brooks Mitchell (1994), the founder of many companies, including Aspen Tree Software, was featured in an August 16, 1993, *Forbes* magazine article entitled "Slouches Make Better Operators" (Oliver, 1993). Dr. Mitchell's insight revealed that too many employers try to find the "right" person based on the expectations of how the interviewer might prefer a candidate to respond to questions, rather than the actual behaviors of the most effective employees within the organizations. Finding out that the very best operators for the telephone company were prone to watch a great deal of television, the quest for clients of Aspen Tree Software became not the replication of a managerial ideal, but rather the replication of the best employees. Pursuing such nonobvious antecedents allowed clients of Aspen Tree Software to reduce turnover and save costs. One recent example in education came from the award-winning school system of Wayne Township in Indianapolis, Indiana. This nationally recognized school system serves a part of the city of Indianapolis that has high levels of poverty and a population that uses more than 40 native languages—yet it consistently improves student achievement. As the school system staff explored their own antecedents of excellence, they found that improvements in bus behavior on the long morning rides were strongly associated with improvements in reading performance. Similarly, they found that increases in student writing were associated with improvements in student scores in mathematics and science, though few math and science teachers regarded student writing as part of their core responsibilities.

Success in the learning quadrant depends on the definition of the antecedents of excellence, and consultants add the greatest value when they find nonobvious antecedents. Sometimes the causes themselves are unusual and unclear, best identified by someone with an outside perspective. At other times, the causes may be clearer, but the measurements must be innovative. One of the least effective measurements, commonly engaged in by organizations of all sorts, is the "delivery" measurement, in which the leadership assumes that the delivery of training, programs, technology, or some other intervention will automatically be associated with a cause. When leaders assume that mere delivery is an antecedent of excellence, they fall victim to the binary effect, in which there are only two levels of measurement: one or zero, delivered or not delivered, excellent or wretched, on or off. Just as results take place along a continuum of results, so invariably do causes.

The exploration of the variability of causes can be taken to multiple levels. For example, a binary measurement could answer the question, "Did he buy a health club membership?" The answer is either yes or no, but a "yes" answer sheds little light on the number of times the member actually visited the health club. Even the number of visits sheds little light on the length of the visit, and the length of the visit sheds little light on the efficiency, effectiveness, and appropriateness of the workout. Many organizations have invested millions of dollars in customer relations management (CRM) database systems, but there are substantial questions as to the relationship between delivery of those exceptionally complex and expensive systems and organizational results (Rigby & Ledingham, 2004). It is not that CRM systems—or, for that matter, health club memberships or training programs—cannot be appropriately defined as antecedents of excellence. Rather, it is that these variables require nuance, analysis, and measurement.

In this respect, one of the most valuable tools the external consultant offers is deliberately naïve observation. Some people ridicule the notion that leading consulting firms, such as McKinsey & Company, should be able to collect large fees for the work of 25-year-old consultants with liberal arts degrees. It is, in fact, not only their database of experience with companies, but also their willingness to make systematic, massive, and deliberately naïve observations that allows McKinsey or any other consulting organization to address fundamental organizational needs (Raisel, 1999). Only through the identification and refinement of the antecedents of excellence can the consultant add long-term value to the client and to the consulting organization.

Whereas the lower right-hand quadrant, "Learning," represents opportunity, the upper right-hand quadrant, "Leadership," hardly represents organizational nirvana. In a competitive environment, the work required to maintain good results, combined with deep understanding of the antecedents of excellence, is just as challenging (if not more so) as the work required to get there. When results are high, complacency can set in, and it is easy to complete the cycle from the upper right-hand quadrant, "Leading," back to "Luck," and a repetition of the worst part of the cycle, "Losing." One of the most challenging parts of working with a high-performing organization is the deliberate creation of dissatisfaction. Challenging complacency and, in the words of John Kenneth Galbraith, "afflicting the comfortable," is tough; very high-performing organizations tend to characterize their success with the tautological expression, "We're good because we are who we are." This may make for great corporate sloganeering, but it hardly provides a formula for sustained excellence.

This may explain why one of the least helpful things that can happen to any organization is to be used as a paragon of success in a best-selling business book. More than 20 years ago, the first business blockbuster, In *Search of Excellence* (Peters & Waterman, 1982), sold more than 3 million copies. Nevertheless, the excellent companies featured in the book have met a variety of fates: some, such as People's Express, are no longer in existence; others, such as IBM, had to survive near-death experiences before they were able to revive their fortunes. IBM, the successful survivor today, is not the same organization it was in 1982. There is a thin line between effectiveness and arrogance and a only a short distance between competitiveness and complacency.

Defining Client Expectations

Although the concept of a focus on results and the antecedents of excellence may be very clear to you, it is essential that we maintain a focus on what client expectations really are. To beat the drum once more, *it's all about the client*. The client's expectations are invariably framed in light of previous consulting experiences. Therefore, the needs analysis (Appendix A) asks the client to detail major consulting engagements and other major client initiatives over the past three years. This is a critical conversation. Although some clients may suspect you of gathering intelligence on your competitors, the reason for your inquiry is to learn from the client's successes and disappointments with other client-consulting relationships. Some clients are reluctant to hold this discussion, fearing that favorable talk about other consulting companies may put you off, or that negative talk about other consultants will be a red flag. It is therefore essential that this conversation take place in an atmosphere of professionalism, confidentiality, and safety. It might be useful to ask clients what their best consulting experience has been, either in this organization or at other organizations, so that the clients are free to identify the elements of an engagement that over time have been associated with great success. If ever there was a time for deliberately naïve listening and observation, this is it. Be quiet and let the client speak.

Listen for essential elements of effective relationships, such as meeting commitments, dealing with mistakes, punctuality, and accuracy. Listen also for the nuances as to value-added elements of a client-consultant relationship, such as building capacity, building personal and organizational knowledge, and other elements of services that may not have been obvious in the contract, the engagement, or the consulting organization that provided the services. For example, if a client talks about technology insights provided by a marketing firm, the marketing insights provided by a law firm, or legal insights provided by a technology firm, that client's appetite for broad-based expertise and wide organizational applicability should be evident. If the client speaks of personal relationships, whether associated with social and athletic events or family celebrations, it is a hint that this client resonates with the human dynamics of your interactions, not merely with the services that you will render. Whereas one client may regard a birthday card or congratulations on the birth of a child as an inappropriate intrusion into personal matters, another client may feel slighted if such events are overlooked. Unfortunately, these are issues that cannot be addressed with a direct question; "Would you like a birthday card?" simply doesn't work. Rather, discerning these preferences and attitudes requires a degree of empathy and resonance, emotional intelligence skills that can come only from thoughtful listening, patient observation, and inferences drawn from the stories a client tells (Goleman, 1998). As with the rest of the needs analysis, the hours you invest in listening to client stories of successful and unsuccessful engagements in the past will yield an enormous amount of information about the essential ingredients of your future relationship.

The needs analysis focuses on the entire engagement, a relationship that may include many on-site meetings, presentations, and work sessions. For each of these visits, the needs analysis should be reviewed using the pre-engagement conference (Appendix B). This conference not only confirms the logistical details for each trip, but also reviews critical understandings for what the client will regard as a successful engagement. Great consulting engagements can be undermined by the consultant's failure to attend to details. The consultant may expect that the work day begins at 9:00 a.m., but in the culture of some organizations, that is about two hours late. A consultant who is responsible for making a presentation to the client's employees may unwisely assume that the client will organize the event for optimal adult learning, but such an assumption is almost always unwarranted. The number of times when meeting participants have said, "I don't know why I'm here; I was just told to show up" far outnumber those times when every participant arrives at the meeting fully informed and fully engaged.

Even such obvious issues as the physical comfort of meeting participants cannot be taken for granted. Some clients are masterful at this—Phillip Gore's role as host of California leadership training programs is a notable example—but others are indifferent. True horror stories include a client's expectation that employees would have no problems sitting for hours on end on chairs without backs; the use of a facility in which the participant-to-restroom ratio exceeded 100 to 1; the use of a 5-foot by 5-foot screen for an audience of more than 500 people; and last-minute changes in hotels, agenda times, and cities that were made without coordination between the client and consultant. Assume nothing, and double-check every detail.

The pre-engagement conference also provides the opportunity to define success in the client's terms. Although the consultant must, clearly, have the ultimate goal defined by the needs analysis and contract, each separate meeting or event involving face-to-face contact is an opportunity either to reinforce or to undermine the success of the engagement and the relationship.

Morale, Relationships, and Emotional Intelligence

The consulting field is alluring to many people because of its apparent lack of organizational politics. "I don't have a boss, I just do my job, and then I go home," or so the consulting mythology goes. In fact, you do have a boss. The boss is not the client alone; in the words of psychoanalyst and social philosopher Erich Fromm, you are your own "most stern taskmaster" (Fromm, 1976). Some consultants believe that their work will be judged solely on the quality of their work, when in fact, the quality of work and its relationship to organizational results can be a matter of interpretation and ambiguity. Even the way in which you deliver results will have an emotional component to it, and that fact must be recognized (Caruso & Salovey, 2004).

There is inevitably an emotional component in the work of consultants. In some cases, it is because you are working side by side with employees, frequently doing similar work, yet with strikingly different levels of pay and benefits. In some cases, consultants receive substantially more reward for the same work than in-house employees do; this easily creates resentment and anger, not to mention incentives for employees to undermine the consultant's work. In other instances, consultants are brought in as a mechanism to provide short-term labor that is less costly than that of employees, particularly when benefits such as medical care and stock options—perquisites of employees but not outside consultants—are taken into account. Whether the economic advantage favors or disfavors the consultant, whether work rules are more or less stringent, whether relationships are tight or loose, there is an emotional component to the consultant-client relationship that must be recognized. The pretense that work relationships are only about work is an illusion.

In their book, *The Emotionally Intelligent Manager* (2004), researchers David R. Caruso and Peter Salovey suggest four critical emotional intelligence skills for managers. They are equally apt for every consultant:

- Identifying how all key participants feel, themselves included
- Using these feelings to guide the thinking and reasoning of the people involved
- Understanding how feelings might change and develop as events unfold
- Managing to stay open to the data of feelings and integrating them into decisions and actions

The issue is not whether feelings should be relevant to decision making; the fact is that every individual and group decision is a reflection of a complex web of information, and emotions are as much a part of that information as any other data source. In a particularly important warning to consultants and organizational leaders alike, the authors note:

> *What most self-help gurus fail to understand is that introspection and reflection can lead to worsening mood and can result not in insight but in feelings of depression and shame. Awareness is certainly an important component of emotional intelligence, but it must be accurate and not obsessive. We must know how we feel and be able to label our feelings appropriately if we wish to better understand ourselves and others [36].*

Some clients will not respond well to questions about feelings, particularly from a consultant whom they expect to be a source of objective information. Nevertheless, an effective consulting relationship is not possible without a consideration of all information available, including the potentially volatile feelings of the stakeholders in the client organization.

The Real Client

One of the most sensitive topics in the needs analysis is the discovery of the real client. It is not unusual for a single element of the organization, such as the operations division or purchasing department, to be the initial and primary contact with consultants. This is particularly true when the selection of consultants begins with a request for qualifications (RFQ), followed by a formal request for proposal (RFP). The foot in the door results from an exchange of emails, conversations, and other information between the consultant and that department. However, the real client—the one who must be satisfied in order for the consultant to have a satisfactory engagement and the potential for a long-standing relationship—may include a group of people in a completely different part of the organization. The identification of the real client requires direct questions and clear answers. Among these might be:

- Who will sign the final contract?
- Who will approve the criteria for work?
- Who will create specifications for work?
- Who will approve change orders?
- Who will evaluate the work at the conclusion of the engagement?

When the answers to these questions turn out to be either unclear or, not uncommonly, people with whom the consultant is completely unfamiliar, the result is very likely to be deep misunderstanding, wasted energy, and high degrees of dissatisfaction by both client and consultant.

Client-Centered Engagements

A leader in any enterprise, from the single-person consulting firm to a global corporation, must have a well-developed ego. Indeed, Harvard Business School professor Rosabeth Moss Kanter (2004) claims that confidence is a key ingredient in realizing and sustaining successful leadership. Even the most successful consultants can be seduced by the notion that they are saviors when, in fact, they may be Svengali. The most dangerous illusions arise when consultants start to believe their own press. Enthusiastic comments from a reader or listener that "you changed my life" or "you transformed this entire organization" are, to be sure, ear candy to most people. Uncritical acceptance of these laurels, however, can lead the consultant and the client to three very dangerous conclusions.

The first is that only the consultant—and often that means only a particular person within the consulting organization—has the right touch to achieve the client's objectives. This leads to a cult of personality that not only undermines the client's ability to build internal capacity, but also undermines the consulting organization. The ideas that might have influenced the client for the better become less important than the personalities of the individuals involved. The subordination of ideas to personality virtually ensures that lasting change will be impossible, and that the good results will disappear with the vapor trail of the consultant's departing airplane.

The second dangerous conclusion is that a measurement of a consultant's effectiveness is the enthusiasm with which he or she is embraced by the client. In fact, change of any sort is, by its very nature, a rejection of prevailing practices. Change represents an emotional loss to individuals who are invested in the status quo, and change may represent a threatening shift in the balance of organizational power (Kotter, 1996). When popularity becomes the standard by which a consultant's recommendations are evaluated, vague reassurances will prevail over the tough challenges that are essential to continuous improvement.

The third dangerous conclusion of consultant-centered engagements is that the consultant must always be the unchallenged expert. Clients feed this presumption when they assume that a consultant who is, in fact, highly expert in one field is therefore expert in every field. When the consultant is articulate, influential, and confident, it is easy to perpetuate the myth. After all, the client is paying for expertise, solutions, and confidence. The subtle message given to the consultant is, "Never let them see you sweat." It requires more bravado than bravery for a consultant to have a slick rejoinder to every challenge and leave every meeting with each participant bowled over by the consultant's confidence. More courage is required for the consultant to acknowledge the complexity of client challenges. This is the consultant who is willing to say openly, "This is exceedingly difficult and I need to think about this and ask my colleagues for advice about this challenge. We have an extensive knowledge base of our experience with other clients, but I don't want to give you false confidence. I won't lie to you—there are no easy and immediately apparent pat answers. This is going to take some real work and deep reflection, but I'm confident that together we can frame some alternatives and develop an effective solution." At the end of the most successful engagements, clients can say, "We did it ourselves." The best consultants may provide insight, ideas, challenges, and expertise. But consulting stars also give the client the confidence and capacity to sustain the work of the consultant long after the engagement has ended.

Figure 1.3 provides an example of how consulting effectiveness can be evaluated. The left hand column includes criteria for evaluating consulting engagements from the initial client contact through an analysis of the consultant's impact on client results. The other columns describe a range of performance from wretched to superlative. This is only an abbreviated example. You will want to create a matrix that is directly relevant to the needs of your clients.

Now that we have established that the client's needs are primary—from the beginning of the needs analysis through the completion of the engagement—we will consider the various ways in which consultants deliver their services. Some fundamental choices face every consultant regarding specialties, expertise, research, and most of all, which engagements to accept and decline. That is the subject of Chapter 2.

Figure 1.3		Analyzing Consulting Effectiveness		
	Exemplary	**Proficient**	**Progressing**	**Not Meeting Standard**
Initial Contact	Client contacted us either: 1. Because we had crafted a compelling proposal; even though they didn't know us, the power of our ideas beat the competition; *or* 2. Because they liked and trusted us because of an article, speech, or other contact, and they transferred the impression of competence in one area to generalized trust and competence; *or* 3. They checked our references, which were uniformly stellar.	Client contacted us because we are among "the usual suspects" when one thinks of standards, assessment, and accountability. They had some confidence in our abilities and were also referred by a trusted colleague.	Client needed to get the job done and we were at the right place at the right time—not a particularly planned or purposeful match.	We were in the phone book before "Zachary."
Scope of Services	Comprehensive services, including needs analysis, market planning, assessment models and creation, accountability system, staff development to support the entire project, leadership consulting at the executive and board level, and continuous hotline support.	Consistent professional development with follow-up to determine the impact of our work. The professional development we presented was specifically linked to a needs analysis.	Products and/or services was based on client's self-determined needs analysis, with little or no input from us. Unstructured follow-up.	Hey—just fill the date on the calendar. It's all "drive-by staff development" anyway.
Agreement	Crystal-clear written agreement, but with some flexibility to meet changing client needs.	Letter of agreement (LOA) that is clear and understood by all parties. We deliver what they expected, and perhaps a little more.	Standard LOA—no more, no less.	What LOA?
Communication with Client	Frequent (at least every two weeks) contact between the consulting firm and client leaders, as well as multitiered contacts with staff and administrators. We are the trusted information brokers who not only provide outside advice to the client, but also provide insight on internal communications (and lack of it) to the client. CEOs, COOs, union representatives, staff, and administrators are all comfortable talking with us at a heart-to-heart level.	Clear communication with client leaders who influence specific plans and place our work in broader context. Follow-up that goes way beyond smile sheets and includes the impact of our work. Free, open, and honest two-way communication. Both sides fill information requests promptly, completely, and courteously.	We got the information we asked for after several requests.	"Why do you need our assessment information anyway? Just do the speech and get out of here."
Teamwork in the Firm	Flawless coordination, with detailed schedule of dates and commitments monitored by the project coordinator. Each team member is chosen for his or her expertise and background and feels totally confident that his or her special attributes contribute uniquely to the project.	A team of qualified and competent consultants meets the client's expectations, perhaps a little more. Invoices and receipts were submitted in a timely manner in	One or two consultants tried to do everything, including some things beyond their expertise. Invoices went out late, but at least they were sent out.	They wanted a warm body, and we delivered a warm body. Of course, we didn't get paid, because communication between the consultant and operations/finance was nonexistent.

(continues)

Figure 1.3 (Continued)	Analyzing Consulting Effectiveness		
	Exemplary	**Proficient**	**Progressing**	**Not Meeting Standard**

	Exemplary	Proficient	Progressing	Not Meeting Standard
Teamwork in the Firm	Team members communicate with each other on an Internet or intranet Web site specifically for that client, and information gained by one team member is immediately and automatically shared with other team members. All team members share the successes and challenges. Communication with operations/ finance was perfect, with the client happily paying for the value it received and the firm billing with total accuracy because all receipts and documents were in order and submitted on time.	accordance with the LOA and internal policies.		
Impact on Client Stakeholders	Measurable increases in student achievement, as well as in the professional practices that are the documented antecedents of excellence. Testimonials and case studies from staff and administrators confirm the impact of our work.	Follow-up information that allows the consulting firm to draw some analytical inferences about the impact of its work.	If we ask for it enough times, they'll share some data, but they don't have much of an idea of what causes good or poor performance.	Either the audience liked it or they didn't; what else is there?

CHAPTER 2

Delivery: Defining Your Services

Specialist or Generalist?

Becoming an Expert

The Role of Research

Declining Engagements

The range of consulting services is breathtaking in its variety. Some consultants market themselves as organizational trouble-shooters, providing general advice on almost anything that clients need; others are exceptionally specific about the scope of their work, supporting very specific needs in particular industries. In this chapter, I suggest that all consultants take the time to define clearly what they will do and, of equal importance, what they will not do.

Specialist or Generalist?

Although many successful consultants have developed careers based on their general ability to solve a wide variety of organizational problems, my personal conviction is that people who are attempting to launch their careers are best served by identifying a specialty. The specialty selected should reflect not only the consultant's personal expertise, but also the consultant's commitment to remain at the cutting edge of that particular field. I am a voracious reader, typically consuming a book and several journals every week. (What else can I do while waiting at airports?) Nevertheless, every few weeks someone will say, "Of course you have seen . . ." and refer to a particularly noteworthy article or book. The honest answer is that, no, I had not seen it and I was not even aware of it, despite my diligent attempts to remain well read in my field. Clients expect me to be an expert—not only a person who conducts research and has access to research, but also a person who is intimately familiar with research in the field. When I am asked a question and can provide a response supported by three independent research citations off the top of my head, it helps prove to clients that they have hired an expert, justifies their perception of me personally as an expert, and builds their confidence in me. The broader the claimed field of expertise, the less likely it is that their perception can be justified.

How do you select a specialty? Perhaps the best way is to use a combination of factors, including market demand, personal interest, and demonstrable personal expertise (Figure 2.1). I have a personal passion for blues piano music but, alas, lack expertise in this area. Moreover, even as I attempt to develop a rudimentary level of proficiency in the blues, there is unlikely to be a sufficient market demand to allow me to support my family in this endeavor. Conversely, there are areas of very significant market demand, such as supply chain management in global manufacturing enterprises, but I lack the expertise to even begin to understand the complexities of that field. Only when market demand, personal passion, and expertise coincide is there the opportunity for a meaningful and productive consulting career. This analysis is similar to that advocated by Jim Collins of *Good to Great* fame (2001), who suggested that the three interlocking circles of the economic engine, "best in the world" capability, and personal passion were the keys to long-term organizational success.

Finally, the case for specialization is based on the potential to dominate a market that you help to create, rather than becoming a competitor in a market that is already flooded with competition. Huge markets—the health care industry, city government, high technology—may seem appealing because of their sheer girth, but the consulting services to these markets are also dominated by individuals

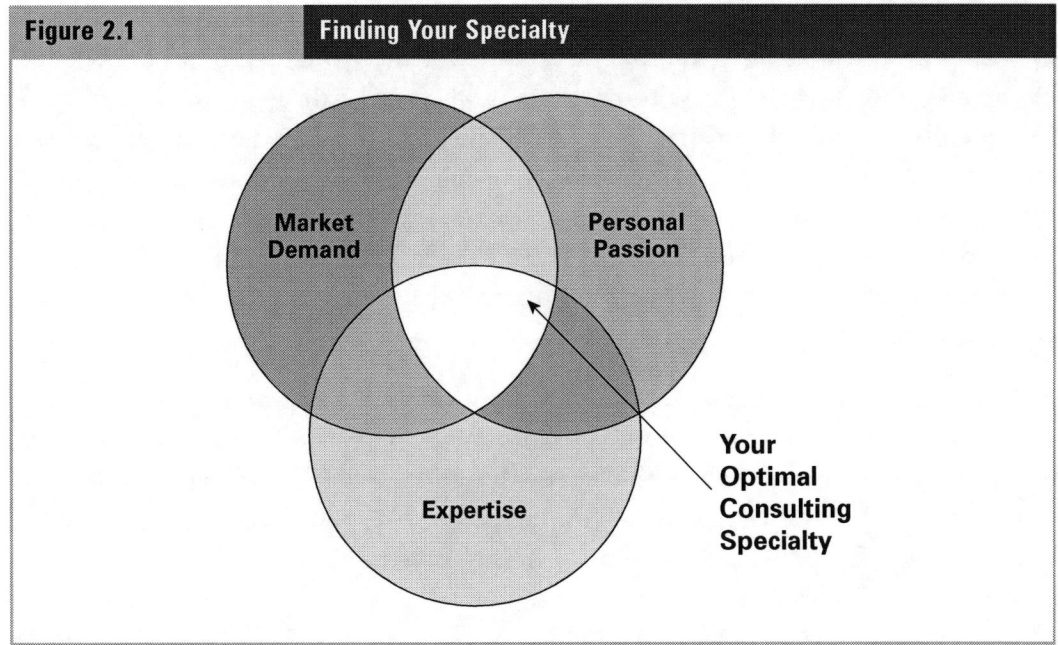

Figure 2.1 **Finding Your Specialty**

Market Demand

Personal Passion

Expertise

Your Optimal Consulting Specialty

and organizations that have extensive experience and connections. If you are launching your consulting career, now is the time to differentiate yourself. This is the "blue ocean" strategy—a term coined by W. Chan Kim of the Boston Consulting Group and a professor of Strategy and International Management at Insead in Fontainebleau, France; and Renée Mauborgne, also of Insead (2004). "Blue oceans denote all the industries not in existence today—the unknown market space, untainted by competition. In blue oceans, demand is created rather than fought over. There is ample opportunity for growth that is both profitable and rapid" (pp. 77–78). Whereas the red-ocean strategy focuses on engaging and defeating the competition, blue-ocean strategy suggests that there is more opportunity in creating uncontested market space. Rather than defeat the competition, blue-ocean consultants render the competition irrelevant. Rather than exploiting existing demand, blue-ocean consultants create and capture new demand. Although Chan and Mauborgne intend their theory to apply to global corporate strategy, their insights have equal applicability to a single-person consultancy.

Becoming an Expert

The Latin root *expertus* gives an important clue as to the real meaning of the word *expert*, because the same Latin term provides the linguistic foundation for both *experience* and *experiment*. Thus, the expert is not merely a person who knows a lot about something, nor is it someone who has a great deal of experience in an area. Rather, an expert, in the truest sense of the word, combines knowledge, experience, and the willingness to create new knowledge through experimentation. Consultants who add the greatest value to clients, and thus are most in demand, are those for whom every client engagement is an opportunity to contribute vital information, develop greater experience, and (as a result of the application of knowledge and experience) develop new insights. These new insights will continue the cycle of value-added consulting throughout the present engagement and for every successive client that the consultant serves.

Let us consider each of these three important parts of expertise. First, you must develop specialized knowledge. This does not necessarily mean that you must acquire an advanced degree—we all know of experts without degrees, and people with advanced degrees who lack expertise. But specialized knowledge does involve a broad and deep understanding of whatever your field regards as results, and also a clear conception of the antecedents of excellence—the measurable actions that are associated with achievement of results. Consulting is an almost wholly unregulated field. Although the public expects, rightly or wrongly, a certain degree of expertise by those who hold a professional designation, such as certified public accountant, attorney at law, chartered financial analyst, or medical doctor, consultants typically must establish their credibility with performance rather than credentials.

Second, the expert will build on specialized knowledge with experience. We expect most physicians not only to diagnose what is wrong with us, but also to use their expertise to help us get better. As they gain experience, their ability to detect subtle variations in patient symptoms becomes sharper and their diagnostic abilities become more nuanced. The novice database engineer may be able to create a database to client specifications, but the expert can go beyond the stated client need, working on the background of experience with the challenges involved in previous database creation and revision.

Third, the expert must experiment. Although clients might initially recoil at the suggestion that they are the subject of an experiment, world-class consultants, such as Michael Porter (perhaps the leading organizational strategy consultant in the world) routinely use client experiences to test hypotheses, gather data, refine theories, and challenge prevailing assumptions. As a result of this experimental approach, a symbiotic relationship emerges between consultant and client, with the client benefiting from the consultant's growing expertise, and the consultant benefiting from lessons learned with each engagement.

The Role of Research

The world of research is typically divided into quantitative and qualitative approaches, with the former subject to numerical measurement and the latter characterized by narrative description. A combination of these approaches usually yields the most productive insights for both clients and consultants. Quantitative measurement is often regarded as the most objective form of research, and numerical values are easily assigned to variables such as revenues, productivity, or time. Even such "soft" measurements as employee satisfaction and customer perceptions take on the appearance of quantification when surveys require respondents to use numerical values to describe their agreement or disagreement with a statement (for example, responding on a scale of 1 to 10 to such propositions as, "I am very satisfied with my new car" or "My supervisor gives me helpful feedback"). There is great danger, however, in excessive reliance on quantitative measurement. When I taught graduate-level statistics courses, I would remind students of two fundamental lessons that would help them when the complexity of statistical analysis seemed overwhelming. First, life is multivariate—never assume that there is only one cause for one effect. Second, not everything can be measured with a number. Knowing that my customer satisfaction or employee engagement score is 3.5 yields little valuable information unless I have also gathered qualitative information; specifically, narrative descriptions that help me to understand what a "3" or a "4" means to the people who awarded those numbers.

To have widespread applicability, research must be replicable and replicated. Bearing in mind the rule that "life is multivariate," the medical researcher studying the effects of smoking on human health in the 1950s might have been perplexed to find the associations between the use of cigarettes and the development of lung cancer to be inconsistent, particularly among those who made their living working in coal mines, inhaling industrial asbestos, or hauling waste from uranium processing plants. Cancer cells would not be clearly flagged with the cause that generated them, and the presence of multiple carcinogens might cloud the true danger of tobacco. Only when the observations were repeated in a large sample of people with dissimilar environments could the now-famous warning of the Surgeon General be made: "Cigarette smoking is hazardous to your health." Similarly, a business consultant studying employee engagement might be unable to draw many conclusions when the pay, bonuses, economic environment, office political climate, and leadership techniques of supervisors all have an impact on employee attitudes. Nevertheless, after making many repeated observations in different employment environments, the consultant and researcher can start to draw inferences about the relative impact of each of these various factors.

Because research is a critical part of both the individual consulting engagement and the insights required by the client, it is essential that consultants have an agreed-upon research protocol for every engagement. More than one consulting engagement has been undermined by the client's refusal to give the consultant the information necessary to conduct meaningful research. Of course it is impossible to provide an exhaustive list of all the data a consultant may wish to have, but the general rule is that you must start with detailed information about client-defined results. If your objective is to improve revenues and profits, you must have access to detailed financial information. If your objective is to improve employee engagement, you must have access to detailed information about employee policies, compensation, and benefits; evaluation processes; supervisory practices; employee training; previous surveys of employee attitudes; and every other bit of data surrounding employee engagement. If your objective is to improve student achievement in a school system, you must have access to detailed information on test scores, curriculum, teaching practices, and other factors surrounding student achievement. If your objective is to improve supply chain management, you must have detailed information on every element of the supply chain, including vendor information, inventory data, manufacturing requirements, and cost structure. As obvious as these requirements may seem, clients are sometimes surprised by and resistant to requests for what they regard as proprietary and confidential information.

Client resistance to full disclosure is understandable. Nevertheless, the absence of clear and candid communication can greatly undermine a client engagement. It is therefore essential that the consultant outline the scope of information needs early in the engagement process. Just as a physician must ask prying questions of the patient—including questions that may embarrass or make the patient uncomfortable—the effective consultant must know where the organizational bodies are buried, learn about past triumphs and failures, and examine the client's dirty laundry objectively and nonjudgmentally. The consultant seeking to help build teamwork and organizational morale must know, for example, if the organization has had a history of age, race, or sex discrimination. The consultant seeking to help improve financial results must be aware of previous accounting scandals. The consultant seeking to improve student achievement must learn early about previous cheating. Although these problems need not become the focus of the engagement, the effective consultant must know about them and consider that context when designing a course of action.

Just as it can be difficult to uncover organizational dirt, consultants may similarly find it difficult to discover organizational success stories. This is particularly true when the executive responsible for the engagement was not responsible for those successes. In one engagement, for example, I conducted a detailed analysis of the performance of every professional in the organization. I thought the chief executive would be pleased to hear about these organizational "diamonds in the rough," previously unrecognized employees who were doing a terrific job. I was stunned to hear him say, "I wouldn't call those our most effective people," and turned the conversation to people who spoke up at meetings and engaged the boss in conversation. That leader valued loquaciousness over achievement, and this helped me understand the poisonous environment in his organization. Getting results, being effective, and quietly doing one's job were not valued nearly as much as volubility in support of the boss's pet initiatives. This was an environment that elevated politics over performance. Although I was not able to reinforce the executive's stereotypes, I did serve the client's short-term interests by identifying and recognizing excellent performance, and I served the client's long-term interests by making it clear to the board that the leader's notion of "performance" was substantially at variance with reality.

Declining Engagements

You will be defined not only by the engagements you accept, but also by those you decline. Declining engagements requires a relentless focus on your mission and an understanding of the Law of Initiative Fatigue. If you do not have a mission, stop right now and draft a statement that encapsulates your passion—those things that give you and your organization meaning and value. Great mission statements help organizations decide both what to do and what not to do. In *The Daily Disciplines of Leadership* (Reeves, 2002a), I reviewed mission statements that were ponderous, officious, and impenetrable. In the days before I penned this chapter, I asked a roomful of leaders to tell me their mission statement. Perhaps three hands, out of more than 200, went up, so I asked those brave souls to tell me their mission. The first started confidently, then trailed off, as she forgot all but the first few words. It was obvious to all that she was tap-dancing, making up the statement rather than using it as a device for leadership focus. These were hard-working, committed leaders whose frenetic work pace had led them to the brink of exhaustion. They did all that was asked of them and more, but never knew when to say, "Wait—this activity does not support our mission, and therefore we need to respectfully decline it."

In addition to declining engagements for yourself, you must also help clients resist the temptation to take on a never-ending stream of initiatives that promise to address their most urgent needs. Each initiative is born of good intentions, but as they grow in number, each subsequent initiative is ultimately undermined by the Law of Initiative Fatigue (Figure 2.2). I choose my words carefully: this is not

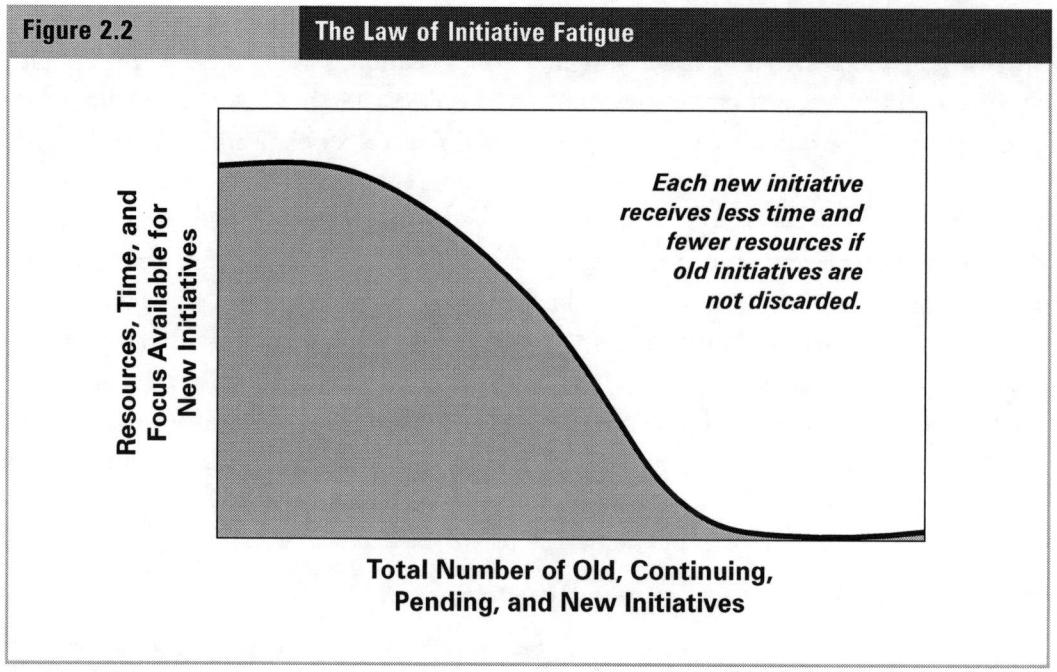

Figure 2.2   **The Law of Initiative Fatigue**

Resources, Time, and Focus Available for New Initiatives

Each new initiative receives less time and fewer resources if old initiatives are not discarded.

Total Number of Old, Continuing, Pending, and New Initiatives

an observation, idea, or gentle suggestion, it's a *law,* and as certain to affect consultants and their clients as are the laws of physics. The Law of Initiative Fatigue states that as the number of new and continuing organizational initiatives increases, the quantity of time, energy, money, and organizational focus will decline.

As the shape of the curve suggests, the decline is imperceptible at first—after all, if two initiatives are working well, a third might be even better. Personal enthusiasm, leadership demands, and sheer adrenaline can sustain these efforts, if only for a while. Ultimately, however, the weight of multiple initiatives undermines organizational effectiveness, and the decline is steep and swift. Organizations are particularly vulnerable to the effects of the Law of Initiative Fatigue when they fail to use their mission to filter out extraneous activities, or when they fail to recognize redundancies in their practices. In my own work, I have found cases in which there were seven redundant initiatives, all purporting to do the same thing, each with its own training program, paperwork, and short-term administrative enthusiasm. It was as if they were decorating a tree with multiple ornaments, but never noticed that the branches were sagging to the breaking point. The legacy of initiative fatigue lasts long after the organization finally stops doing the work; thereafter, personnel greet increasing demands from the hierarchy as just one more piece of junk mail. Even productivity and other necessary initiatives are met with skepticism and cynicism, and a knowing mutter of the mantra for the fatigued, "This too shall pass."

Consultants cannot avoid the Law of Initiative Fatigue. They can only choose whether to contribute to the downward slope of organizational ineffectiveness. To avoid this fate, the best consultants develop expertise based on their own knowledge, deepening experience, and a willingness to apply their experience and knowledge to client work through experimentation, hypothesis testing, and sharing of results. The very best consultants are the ones who can say, "This is not working—let's stop it," and thus be a part of the small minority of voices who will help relieve clients from the burdens of excessive initiatives rather than adding to them. In a world in which consultants are known far more for adding to organizational burdens than for subtracting from them, this may seem counterintuitive and even risky. The first description is true; it is against the predisposition of most consultants, and that is why so few of them do it. The second description, however, is false. The real risk is a reputation for burning clients and their employees with excessive work demands. It is far less risky to be honest and recommend against courses of action, even at the risk of losing an engagement, than to take on every task and embrace every initiative, pursuing short-term gain at the expense of long-term reputation.

The next chapter will apply and also consider counterintuitive, but low-risk, strategies, this time in the field of marketing. Some consulting firms engage in aggressive marketing that is brazenly self-promotional, but Chapter 3 suggests instead marketing strategies that are low in cost, lower in hubris, and very high in effectiveness.

Marketing: Generating Sales without Selling

Readers approach a chapter about the marketing of consulting services from two diametrically opposite points of view. Some think I should simply get to the point: "How do I market my services to the greatest number of people for the maximum amount of money?" Others hesitate to approach the topic, and ask: "How can I sell services that I believe are essential for the public good?"

While some readers wonder *how* they can sell, others wonder *if* they can sell. In the next few pages, I will honor both questions. If you will persist until the end of this chapter, I will tell you the story of how I made the transition—without spending a penny on advertising—from being a breakout speaker to an audience of seven people to giving keynote addresses to tens of thousands of people every year. I said I haven't spent anything on advertising. I have, however, spent a lot of money giving away free services, publications, and ideas. Although I have been burned occasionally by those who steal intellectual property, I have learned the rule of "consulting karma"—the more you give, the more you get.

As you think about the way you will market your professional services, consider the way you react to other professionals as they market their services to you. The very concept of sales and marketing is distasteful to many people who regard themselves as professionals. After all, the most reputable doctors and lawyers don't advertise—indeed, advertising in those professions remains prohibited in some areas and can be interpreted as questionable even where it is permitted. It's the Groucho Marx theory of professionalism. With arched eyebrows and animated cigar, Groucho claimed that he didn't want to be a member of any country club that would accept him as a member. Similarly, we are reluctant to go to a professional who might accept us as a client. Better to be put on a waiting list and suffer the indignities imposed by the overworked, overscheduled, and underappreciated professional rather than get to see a less well-known professional tomorrow. Yes, it's convenient and might even garner us exceptional service, but if it's too easy, then it can't be that good, can it? With these perverse stereotypes, which really are surprisingly prevalent, we can presume that clients place a premium on the hasty and sloppy and reject the careful and attentive, particularly if the former are remote and difficult to engage and the latter advertise and are easily accessible.

Reconciling Sales and Service

The thesis of this chapter is that *you do not have to reconcile sales with service—great professionals do both*. They market and sell their services because they know in their hearts that they are doing the right thing; they also provide great service. Their reputation for service will, in the long run, be their greatest advertisement. Contrary to popular mythology, professionals need not be aloof, indifferent, inaccessible, and mysterious in order to gain the confidence of those they serve. My support for this claim includes my experience as one who both delivers and receives services. In the Boston area, we have access to world-class medical care. My wife and I have been on the receiving end of medical procedures when our doctor paused to share techniques of colleagues from Europe and Asia. These are professionals who publish in the most prestigious research journals and share their knowledge worldwide. Yet the same doctor calls at 9:30 at night just to see how things are going and offer support, or extends an office call by 15 minutes just to answer the questions of a nervous patient. Doctors Reiser, Zanni, Ingraham, and Odiet are exceptional not only because of their world-class reputations and personal expertise, but also because they defy the stereotype of the medical professional who is too busy taking care of patients to really take care of patients. These professionals stand out because the stories of their opposite numbers are legion: the preoccupied surgeon who operates on the wrong body part or, more commonly, dismisses patients from the hospital prematurely; the inattentive lawyer who puts the wrong name on the document or sends the right document to the wrong address; the technology consultant who fixes the computer problem but fails to document how the repair was made and thus ensures an expensive recurrence; the mechanic who blithely says, "This will be a very delicate procedure," but is reluctant (like some surgeons) to discuss the costs and benefits of the proposed repair. The careless attitude conveyed by their actions is, "Hey, you want a different professional? Go ahead, try to find one." More frequently than we care to admit, we accept poor service, persuaded that we have few if any alternatives.

So here you are, building a consulting practice. How do you balance the scale? If your service is "too good," will you look desperate for business if you advertise? If your service mirrors that of the indifferent professionals with whom we have all dealt as clients, will you risk alienating current and future clients? My strong advice is this: Do not try to find a balance. You will never—not ever—go wrong by providing exceptional service. Forget about the criticism that great service will taint your reputation as being appropriately elusive. (Playing hard-to-get might have worked in junior high, but it's not a good professional strategy.) You want to be the "Dr. Reiser" of the consulting world? Call clients at home at 9:30 at night just to see how they are doing. You want to be the "Dr. Odiet" of the consulting world? Give your clients extra time, even when you think you should abruptly move on to your next appointment. You want to be the "Dr. Ingraham" or "Dr. Zanni" of the consulting world? Answer every question from clients, no matter how naïve, intrusive, clueless, or skeptical. I would like to immodestly add that if you aspire to be the "Doug Reeves" of the consulting world, then you should return every email and call, even from people who will never buy a single book or contract a single engagement. Give the local library, nonprofit organization, religious group, or school the same quality for which another client will pay $10,000. Some day, when you least expect it, they will tell someone else about the extra time you spent to help them, and that story will spread, enhancing your reputation as a consultant. Even if it doesn't, you did the right thing, and that knowledge will sustain you during some very long days and nights. If anyone thinks that your service was "too good" and that your availability to help them was unbecoming of a busy professional, well . . . that is a risk worth taking.

Two incidents that illustrate this point stand out in my mind. The first occurred at a recent national convention where I was a keynote speaker. I have a rule about not promoting my own work before audiences. I'll recommend colleagues and even competitors, but I don't talk about my own books and services. From the audience came the comment, "You are selling yourself short—your group, the Center for Performance Assessment, provides exceptional training and support, and I'm living proof of how effective you have been . . . ." That brief comment from the floor was worth many thousands of dollars of advertising and was far more authentic than the typically contrived endorsement.

The second occurred when I was sitting in a physician's office. Without going into graphic detail, it is fair to say that I was not wearing my bowtie or much of anything else. The doctor, who was seeing me for the first time, asked, "You wouldn't by any chance have given a speech recently in San Francisco, would you?" In fact, I had. "Well, I just saw a patient who was in the audience and remarked how the speaker took time afterwards to provide time and attention—it really made a difference in her life. When I saw your name on the chart, I wondered if it was you." I still don't know who the mystery patient was, but I do know that every moment devoted to client service, whether in person after a presentation or during a late-night email, is time well spent. There is no quantifiable return on investment for these moments, but they represent more of what I aspire to be than any financial statement.

How Can You "Sell" a Vital Service?

You believe in what you do. Whether you help fight computer viruses; train telephone service representatives; coach corporate executives; help small businesses survive; help teaching, medical, or legal professionals improve their skills; or provide any number of other consulting services, you know that you are doing good and important work. You feel a moral obligation to provide this work: it is literally so important that you would do it for free—and, unfortunately for your family's bank account, you do that more frequently than you care to admit. Ultimately, you must address the moral and business issue of how you sell a vital service.

The most direct answer to this dilemma is that if you fail to sell your services, you will not provide them to those most in need. In my case, I have resolved this issue by the application of religious principles that cross many different traditions, including tithing and "first fruits." Muslims and Buddhists, Jews and Christians, humanists and Hindus, people of many different faiths and of no religious conviction at all know intuitively that we benefit most when we help others. At the same time, we must recognize that our ability to help others is dependent upon our own survival. Thus, total self-denial is as bad as total self-absorption: in neither case can we provide long-term sustenance to family and society. Although the concept of tithing—giving away a 10 percent share—may not be perfect, it is a reasonable starting point for balancing service with self-preservation. In my case, I provide about 100 engagements every year, and 12 of those are done for free or at a minimal cost that barely covers expenses. For the other 88 engagements, the fees I charge clients are, I think, appropriate and necessary, though clearly at the high end of the market. This fee structure allows me to earn a good living, but also allows me to provide free and low-cost services to clients in need, provide excellent pay and benefits to my employees, and fund research and development that will help both my clients and my company in the years ahead. I have made a very deliberate decision to create higher gross revenue (fees received from clients) and lower net revenues (income earned by me) in order to create an organization that has long-term sustainability.

There are very successful competitors in my field who do no free engagements and who invest not a single penny in research and development. Indeed, many of them quote my research, frequently without attribution. In the short term, they are more economically successful than I am. In any equation but the shortest of terms, however, their avarice will give way to my long-term view. What we do in building an organization and investing in research is not charitable; in the words of Nobel laureate Milton Friedman, it is "enlightened self-interest" (Friedman & Friedman, 1980).

This business model has worked well for my business and my conscience. In my religious tradition, there are many forms of charity, but the highest form is that which provides opportunities for other people so that they no longer need to rely on charity. Thus, the creation of jobs and the growth of an enterprise is not merely a western version of capitalism, but the establishment of an opportunity for a people and families to earn a living and become self-sufficient. Consultants are entrepreneurs, and whether you employ one person or one thousand, you are, at least in my view, engaging in an honorable, decent, and moral act. The marketing of your services is not an act of greed, but a creative enterprise in which each dollar of revenue simultaneously serves the interests of clients, employees, and business owners.

Dealing with Limited Client Resources

Whatever consulting services you offer, you will inevitably encounter clients who claim that the price of your services exceeds their budget. This will happen with profit-making clients who have multibillion-dollar budgets (and profits), with nonprofit organizations that cannot meet their next payroll, and with public organizations that are flush with cash but are hounded by donors and directors to be good stewards of their resources. You may occasionally encounter a client who says, "Money is no object—just get the job done and pay no attention to the cost," but my heartfelt suggestion is that you take careful note of the pharmaceutical, vintage, or hypnotist that induced such a trance, as such a rare mental excursion usually represents a diversion from reality.

Early in my consulting career, I was a complete sucker for poverty pleas, and would do anything to help a distraught client. "I'll cut my fees in half! I'll stay over Saturday to save you air fare! Motel 6 with three roommates? No problem!" Well, *almost* anything to help a distraught client. Then, one day in a cold northwestern state, I noticed something strange. I shared the stage with a competitor who was older and wiser. Accepting the client's plea, I had signed a deeply discounted contract. Now I was on stage, providing services that were as good or, in the view of the client, even better than those of my competitor. But my competitor had established a price and stuck to it—it was more than five times my discounted cost. What had the client done with the money I saved them? Did they feed poor children? Did they balance their budget? Did they pay the health insurance for their staff? No—they paid my competitor who was unwilling to discount his services. Worse yet, news of my "confidential" discount spread like Paul Revere's ride, and every client in the area soon expected the same treatment, at least from me. All so that they could afford my more expensive competitor! I learned a valuable lesson from that engagement. It is better to do an engagement for free than to give a discount, as the discount only establishes your worth in the eyes of the client. Give them services for free, and you are a hero. Give them services at a discount, and you are merely cheap. It is better to send an invoice for $10,000 and then mark it out in your own hand as a donation than to submit an invoice for $500 on a $10,000 job and lamely hope that the discount will be appreciated.

The establishment of criteria for free work will help you discern where you will invest your energies. My free engagements are, in some cases, very strategic—national or regional organizations that will help my business grow. In other cases, however, they are with small local groups that will never result in a single dollar of revenues. They are just the right thing to do.

Ethical Marketing

Whenever you engage in marketing activities, you have three ethical obligations. The first is to your prospective clients. Tell the truth and do what you say you will do.

The second obligation is to your existing clients. Are you promising more to new clients than to those clients who have already given you the benefit of the doubt? This is a continuous challenge for me. As a general rule, I adhere to a strict schedule in which I work from 6:30 or 7:00 in the morning and stop at noon. During the afternoon, I travel to the next client site, respond to hundreds of email and voice mail messages, write articles and books, and, I confess, take an occasional nap. What about the times when a client insists that you stay late? Consider this: You have an ethical obligation not only to that client on that day, but also to the next client on the next day. Are you meeting that obligation when, in your zeal to provide great service, you arrive at the next client site at two in the morning and utterly exhausted? Moreover, you previously told a client of long standing that you had strict limits on the time you could give them. How ethical is it for you to break that limit for a new client? Consulting is a relationship business. How would you feel in a relationship if your longtime friend claimed to be unavailable because it was necessary to meet the needs of a new and more attractive relationship?

The third obligation of ethical marketing is to yourself. Very soon, you will reach a point where—as crazy as this claim may seem right now—it will make little difference to you in financial terms what clients you accept or decline. You won't drive a different car, live in a different house, send your children to a different school, or buy a different suit of clothes. All you have left, as a decision factor, is the person you face in the mirror. That is, at least in my case, a distressingly less attractive image with each passing year in physical terms, but however weathered and worn, it can be an image that is, in the most precise sense of the word, satisfactory. In report card terms, this is neither superior nor outstanding; to continue that universal analogy, it almost certainly falls in the category of students who "need improvement." Nevertheless, in the context of ethical marketing, we should all aspire to be "satisfactory," meeting the needs of others and, ultimately, ourselves. Whatever your marketing techniques—published advertisements, sponsorship of charitable events, favorable mentions on public radio and television, or the other marketing techniques we will address in this chapter—you must consider whether you delivered what you promised. If you can respond to that question in the affirmative, then you have met the third challenge of ethical marketing.

Consulting Karma: The More You Give, the More You Get

I speak to tens of thousands of people every year. Every few days, someone will approach me at a conference or, after an engagement, call or send an email. "I'd like to do what you do," the message starts. It is tempting to be flattered by this, though I have few illusions about the conversation. After all, when a six-year-old looks at a firefighter and says, "I want to be like *you* when I grow up," there is an inestimable measure of awe that the firefighter deserves and I do not. But the messages to me do not contain the subtext of those directed to the firefighter. Rather, the subtext is, "You know, you really don't look so bright and this can't be that hard. You went to a state university and were a middle school teacher, for goodness sake. Surely I can do what you do." And indeed, that is the case. They can do what I do, and so can you. The question, however, is not whether you can do what I do, but rather whether you are willing to do what I have done and continue to do. After publishing 19 books, I still write articles for free—four of them in the past six months. After providing thousands of paid presentations, I still give free keynote speeches and seminars; I recently drove nine hours round-trip to give a 30-minute keynote address. In the past few years, my company has earned almost $20 million in revenues, but we still provide keynotes, seminars, books, handouts, and many other materials for free. Why? Because the rule of consulting karma that worked a dozen years ago still works today: *The more you give, the more you get.* How do you give to the world in a way that will result in consulting karma? Consider these ideas:

- Create a Web site (it's cheap—depending on the host, even free) that gives access to your articles, PowerPoint slides, and answers to frequently asked questions in your field.

- Offer audience members free copies of your materials. Our database has expanded from nothing to almost 50,000 names, all based on business cards that people gave us at public presentations. We have never purchased a single name from a mailing list.

- Publish books and pamphlets and give them away. I didn't start by publishing for Simon & Schuster, Jossey-Bass, ASCD, or any other big-name publisher. I took my manuscript to a local printer and spent the rent money on printing.

- Let every group, from Rotary Clubs to professional associations, from local to national, know that you have a compelling, funny, engaging, entertaining, and informative message. If they want you to travel 200 miles to share your ideas and the short-term payoff is overcooked chicken at 7:30 p.m. or undercooked eggs at 7:30 a.m., the correct answer still is, "I would be delighted."

■ Write, speak, and share because what you have to say is important. As I have told many prospective consultants, do this because it is so important that you would do it for free—because you probably will.

Conference Marketing: From Breakout to Keynote

You have persevered this long, so here is the story I promised. It is the story of my consulting career, of my company, of my transition from a kitchen table in a two-bedroom apartment to a consulting career that has taken me to all 50 states and five continents. While a graduate student, I had provided some free services to a friend and colleague, Stan Scheer. Stan then recommended to a conference sponsor that I receive a speaking slot. The coveted invitation to address a national conference arrived in the mail. Be there at Saturday, 2:00 p.m. We will waive tuition for the conference but, of course, you must pay for your own travel, lodging, and meals, the invitation explained. "This is my big break!," I thought.

I did not realize that Saturday afternoons at national conferences are notoriously unpopular times. Although the room could easily have accommodated 200 people, and I had prepared (at my expense) extensive handouts for that many people, precisely seven—*seven*—people showed up. I could barely contain my disappointment; actually, fury would better have described my emotional state. I spent more than $900 an on airplane ticket and another $300 on two nights in an overpriced hotel room for this, my big chance, and seven people show up?

I had done many free breakout sessions before and I knew that there was a "food chain" of conferences—that you worked your way up from breakout speaker to "featured" presenter to keynote speaker. The process takes years, even decades. Politics, popularity, and luck were all factors in making the transition. Suddenly, teaching seventh-grade math was not looking all that bad as an alternative. But seven people had decided to come to this session and they wanted to hear what I had to say. As 2:00 p.m. loomed, I decided that these seven people deserved my best effort. I spoke to the room as if it were packed to overflowing, as indeed would be the case in future years. I made them laugh, wince, and tear up. I gave them evidence, statistics, case studies, and compelling anecdotes. I answered their questions, made them think, and honored their own ideas. Although I thought I had done my best, I feared that I had just spent the next month's rent on the folly of my own ego. With the few dollars I had left, I wandered down to a coffee shop and not only indulged in the luxury of a quad espresso, but also bought the handmade mug in which it was served.

Today, a dozen years later, I drink my morning tea (no longer able to tolerate the strong stuff) from that same mug. Among those seven audience members was the national conference director of one of the biggest service providers in our industry. The very next year, I was keynoting at that conference. Of the 20 key-noters that this organization used a decade ago, precisely two remain standing, and I am one of them. To this day, I provide one free keynote speech a year to that organization, even though it has changed ownership three times in the intervening years. Although I would like to think that my own competence and hard work have been part of this equation, I also know that success represents the confluence of opportunity, preparation, and luck. Given my single-minded determination, I might have been successful without this particular event, but it might have taken many more years.

I continue to provide free presentations (including breakout sessions) at conferences, even when I am the keynote speaker. Each year I encounter good and thoughtful people who turn down these opportunities, because they want to be paid for each presentation. They are loathe to pay their own expenses. Paying tuition is far beneath them, as it would involve listening to and learning from others. Ten years from now, they will continue to say, "I want to do what you do" and think, "He doesn't look so bright. He went to a state school. He was a school teacher, for goodness sake! Why is he on stage when I am still down here?"

Passion: Saying "I Love What I Do" Every Morning

Loving Your Work

Publishing

Dealing with Rejection

The Reason to Write

Reading to Write

United Airlines loves me and, as much as it is possible for a human to love a corporation, I love them. They have survived the vagaries of the economy and unconscionable terrorist attacks, the loss of their pension plans and the destruction of their equity, yet their employees and executives are (almost) unfailingly pleasant, helpful, and friendly.

I've helped flight attendants with statistics homework and they have helped me make tight connections. I've helped baggage handlers deal with wayward strollers and they have helped me locate wayward cell phones (and iPods, briefcases, laptops, manuscripts, raincoats, and an untold number of other artifacts of the absent-minded professor). I make a point of helping elderly and disabled passengers with luggage, hoping that someone will do the same for my family and friends, and (almost) invariably each kindness is reciprocated with a smile of appreciation. Of course, there was that unpleasant incident when I helpfully picked up a senior citizen's suitcase, intending to help put it in the overhead storage compartment, and was assailed as a thief, but that was an exception.

Back to my elegy to United Airlines: Red Carpet Club concierges from Boston to Chicago to LA greet me by name; flight attendants serve me my favorite drink without asking (perhaps they do that for every passenger who wears a bow tie); captains introduce themselves and offer a flight and weather briefing. They give me peanuts and pretzels, and recently a flight attendant sneaked me a free candy bar from the "buy on board" program. In the world of air travel in the twenty-first century, it doesn't get much better this side of a coast-to-coast ride in a private jet. I give them millions of miles of travel (and, I've calculated, more than a million dollars in business in the last decade) and they give me superior service.

If my affection for an inanimate corporation sounds strange — even alien, particularly to those readers who have recently had bad airline experiences — then imagine how much stronger my feelings are for my clients. For every person who says, "This is a waste of my time and the speaker is a fraud," there are hundreds of times as many people who say, "You changed my life." For every disgruntled seminar participant who writes, "I would have been better off shopping or getting a massage," there are many who say, "I was ready to retire and call it quits, but I have decided to give this job another chance." I recently shared a ride to the airport with Robert Marzano; in the field of public education, he is perhaps the best-selling author and the most thoughtful researcher in the past several decades. When I asked Bob about his growing fame, he said, "All I need to do is go home to realize that I may be famous here, but that doesn't cut much ice at home."

So it is. Thirty minutes before a limo arrives to pick me up for an engagement, I am waiting, with many other parents, to pick up my youngest son from middle school. I don't get to cut in line at Stop 'N Shop, I don't get preferential treatment at Grossman's Delicatessen, and I certainly don't get a better table at Passage to India in Salem, Massachusetts, the only Scottish-Indian restaurant on the planet. But within minutes after these humdrum, quotidian experiences, I am transported to a world in which my words make a difference, in which my research matters, in which my appreciation can sustain tired souls. In every job I have had since my earliest teenage years, I have only wanted to make a difference, and that is what sustains me to this day. I am as passionate about the business of consulting as I was about mowing lawns, trimming hedges, and cleaning up after dogs almost half a century ago. As a young and inexperienced military commander in my early twenties, I literally stood on top of a payroll officer's desk to help my troops get the money their families needed for rent. As a teacher, I labored over every word of student work, taking them more seriously than they knew was possible. As a boss, I challenge my colleagues and give them impossible assignments, knowing that they will rise to the challenge. As a consultant, I put every ounce of credibility on the line to challenge clients, move them out of the comfort zone, and provide them with the incentive that is essential to make a difference for them. That is what sustains me in a schedule that looks like this: Sunday, Boston; Monday, Sacramento; Tuesday, New York, Wednesday, Denver; Thursday, Atlanta; Friday, back to Boston. Flights are late, hotels claim to be out of nonsmoking rooms, taxi lines are long, and rooms for a keynote presentation are overheated and poorly lit. Despite it all, when just a single person stops me in the airport and says, "You made a difference for us," the energizing effect exceeds that of any drug yet developed.

The compulsion to make a difference is, according to a recent series of articles in the *Harvard Business Review,* common to many disciplines (Stewart, 2003). Studies of leaders, in both the for-profit and nonprofit sectors, medical and military professions, and worlds of educators and factory workers, found that all had in common the need to do meaningful work. Passion is the air that successful consultants breathe. When disappointments, client demands, travel delays, and a thousand demands on your time threaten to suck the life out of you, passion will sustain you, infusing psychic, emotional, and physical energy.

Loving Your Work

Ask yourself this question: Do you love what you do so much that you would do it for free? What *do* you do for free? If the answer is fly fishing, playing with children, writing, speaking, or sharing your special skills with other people, then you have gained an important insight into what you can do as a consultant. As a writer, I assert with confidence that I invest as much energy in articles and chapters that do not earn a fee as in those that do. In fact, on a dollar-per-word basis, my most lucrative writing has been for airline magazines (where, I regret to say, the quality of my literary efforts was inversely proportional to the reward). Conversely, I have sweated bullets over articles and op-ed pieces that have, in economic terms, been worthless but which, years after their publication, continue to influence the people who read them; I know this because they tell me about the impact of those carefully chosen words on their careers.

As a former professor of graduate school research classes, I am frequently approached by doctoral students who are in search of the perfect topic for their dissertation research. My advice is always the same: do what you love. Graduate school is too hard and completing a dissertation is too much work to be sustained merely by a commitment to the passions of a graduate school advisor, committee chair, or favorite professor. *You must love what you do,* whether you are a 20-something student or a 70-something fourth-career consultant.

When my mother was 74 years of age, she accepted a six-year-term on the national board of trustees of a charitable foundation. At first, she protested, "If I serve my entire term, I'll be 80 years old!"

"And how old will you be in six years," I asked, "if you don't join this board?" Now, entering her eighty-third year, she is an active member of one national and one international board and recently served as parliamentarian for the national convention of an organization with more than 20,000 members. Born into another era, she would have been handsomely paid for her prodigious leadership and analytical talents. Her payment now is a more valuable currency: the certain knowledge that she makes a difference. I do not think she would trade places with succeeding generations, whose measurement of success is usually expressed in economic terms. She rises with the sun, works out at the gym and in the pool like an Olympic athlete, drives better than the average Boston area commuter, engages in passionate advocacy, studies her latest interest like a smitten student, lectures the unsuspecting listener with overwhelming and comprehensive facts and logic, eats as she pleases, enjoys a gin and tonic, and goes to sleep every night knowing that she made a difference. She would never call herself a consultant, but her life and lifestyle reflect the energy and commitment that this profession requires.

If you wish to succeed as a consultant, ask yourself: Can I see myself accepting a commitment to do this when I'm 82 years old? Am I willing to provide these services during my lifetime even if I never receive a penny? It's easier to use my mother than myself as an example, but the following illustration is relevant. Within the past week, I provided the very same services in five different instances. In one case, the fee was zero; in the other four cases, the fees exceeded $30,000 and the aggregate revenues associated with those clients in the past year exceeded $1 million. I invested as much energy before, during, and after the engagement with zero revenue as for the others. The economic rule for consultants is clear: *Passion precedes profits*. If you take one idea from this book, this is it. Write it down, post it near your computer, write it next to your telephone, and clip it on the credit card you will use for a cash advance to take a taxi when your most recent client is late in paying you. Passion precedes profits. This will sustain you from your kitchen table to the board room.

As you build your consulting career, it will be necessary to build your reputation far beyond your present engagements. Although today's clients may sing your praises, tomorrow's clients do not know that you exist. Thus, your passion must extend not only to the work of the present, but also to the invisible work of the future. One of the best ways to reach out to that intangible world is to publish in the professional journals of your field. In a paraphrase of an idea attributed to both Samuel Clemens and Thomas Edison, writing, genius, and invention are the products not of inspiration but of perspiration. The focus of the rest of this chapter is how you can channel your passion into print. If you have crossed the threshold of passion, then your ideas deserve broad exposure. Now is not the time for modesty. If you truly believe in your ideas, you have a moral obligation to share them. Writing is not an option, it's an obligation. Writing will build your credibility and enhance your consulting career. Most of all, writing will provide the avenue through which you share your insights with the outside world.

Publishing

Words on paper matter. If you want to have credibility as a consultant, you must write articles, monographs, and books. Write because your ideas matter, because you have something to say, and because the very same words that you use in a conversation, seminar, or keynote address will be more persuasive if you have expressed them on the printed page. Easy for me to say after 19 books and a lot of articles—but how do you get your ideas published? It's time for another diversion into true confession.

I'm a mathematician, not a writer. It may come as no surprise to a reader who has persisted thus far that, to be charitable about it, my literary skills are limited. I do not understand simile, metaphor, and irony. I fail to grasp the importance of imagery. I am more persuaded by analysis than by animation, more easily seduced by coefficients than by characterization. When I read Somerset Maugham, Stephen J. Gould, or Thomas Paine, I am consumed by their eloquence. The products of their twenty-first-century counterparts, such as Jon Stewart, Robert Marzano, Debra

Pickering, and Thomas Friedman, frequently remind me of my inadequacies. But I slog on, persuaded that good ideas can overcome bad writing. My most humiliating writing experiences are too numerous to recount in these pages, but they include the day when my freshman English professor reproduced my essay for the entire class—the only piece of student work to receive such special treatment. Paragraph by paragraph, word by word, my 17-year-old efforts were reduced to rubble before my peers. In the movie *The Paper Chase,* the feared Harvard Law School Professor Kingsfield pulls a coin from his pocket and offers it to a student with the words, "Here's a dime. Call your mother and tell her that you won't become a lawyer after all." My early writing experiences could hardly have been worse. "Here's a dime. Call your mother and tell her that you won't become a writer after all."

But wait, the worst is yet to come. I worked hard and learned my lessons, and, however imperceptibly, my writing improved, or so I thought. What one editor would call "ground-breaking research," another would characterize as "not quite right for our readership." One editor would say, "This idea is a major development and needs more exposition," and another editor would counter, "The ideas are interesting, but too dense. We need more ideas, fewer words." "You're a great writer," one editor enthused, "but . . . ," with the following sentences implying that "I wish this were a completely different piece of work."

Dealing with Rejection

Three of my cousins are concert violinists. Brian Johnson, son of my mother's brother, Karl Johnson, played in the White House Marine Strings and became a senior member of the National Symphony in Washington, D.C., before his tragic death in a road-rage incident. His sister, Kay Ellen, played in the orchestra for the Santa Fe Opera. Wendy Richards, daughter of my father's sister, Shirley, was a noted soloist and teacher in her early years as a professional. Wendy would paper the walls of her apartment with rejection letters, reminding her that even the most talented and successful performers must deal with and accept rejection. Though I have not saved all my rejection letters, they could easily wallpaper my home. Successful writers joke about the hierarchy of rejection, knowing that the postcard rejection is superseded by the form letter; which is bettered by a personal, albeit computer-generated, letter; which is outdone by the handwritten postscript claiming, "We really like your work, but it's just not right for us at this time"; which is completely outclassed by an actual critique of an article, with eviscerating comments and suggestions for improvement. Amateurs are offended by such letters, but professionals covet them like gold. Rejection *with reasons?* That's the closest thing to acceptance that many would-be writers will ever see.

There is a food chain to writing, just as there is to speaking. For every multimillion-dollar advance offered to the novelist who dangles a wisp of a concept before a bevy of salivating publishers, there are hordes of writers who would happily pay to see their work in print, yet suffer the indignity of postcard rejections, hoping only to graduate to letters, postscripts, and—dare they hope?—the personalized rejection accompanied by a critique of their work. What do these editors want? How can anyone be that brilliant all the time? Look at that slug who was published last month—do you call that great work? It was pedestrian! It was unexceptional! It did not have my insight, energy, and . . . did I mention insight? So, what do editors really want? It turns out that they are somewhat less superhuman than writers might imagine. Do you really want to get published? Here are the rules:

1. **Meet the deadline.** Miss one, and the editor still trusts you. Miss two deadlines, and trust is broken and you are finished.

2. **Hit the word count.** If the editor said 650 words, she didn't mean 675.

3. **Did you get the part about deadlines?**

4. **Read the magazine.** The *New England Journal of Medicine* doesn't want a profile on Britney Spears, and *Star Magazine* isn't enamored of your most recent statistical analysis. Editors get really cranky when prospective authors are not willing to read the magazine or journal to which they are submitting articles. Do your homework and submit the proper material to an appropriate publisher.

5. **Did I mention the deadline?**

6. **Follow format guidelines.** Your high school English teacher was right—format matters. If the editor wants APA, you love APA. If the editor wants MLA, you love MLA. If the editor likes Chicago, you embrace Chicago. There are many things in this world worth fighting about, but citation style is not one of them.

7. **It is possible that the issue about deadlines has not sunk in, so please return to Rule No. 1.**

8. **Get permission.** Copyright is not just a law, but the right thing to do. If you use other people's intellectual property, it's your responsibility to get permission to use it. This is true whether it's a photograph, and you need written permission from the people pictured to reproduce their images; or a quotation of more than a few words from another copyrighted source. Don't make the editor guess about these matters. Submit signed permission

forms and avoid the embarrassment of having the editor have to ask you for them.

9. **You got the deal about deadlines, right?**

10. **Write in the King's English.** How boring! How unfamiliar! How . . . how . . . well, how correct. Don't get all politically correct on me, now. When I say "King's English," I mean it in the constrictive, creativity-crushing mode that the term suggests. That's right—no contractions ("that is right," not "that's right"), no colloquialisms, no Internet blog abbreviations, no presumptions of familiarity. It is easier for the editor to make you less formal than to transform your informal rambling into formal material for journal readers. Write as if your ideas matter, not as if you are feigning familiarity with a subway acquaintance. If you're *really* good, you won't need to use italics for emphasis or contractions for a conversational tone.

The Reason to Write

At the end of the day, you will write many more articles and books than will be published. You write not because your words will always see the light of day, but because you have something important to say. One reason many writers keep journals is that they simply *must write*. Their ideas take form on paper or on the computer screen, and even if the audience is numbered in single digits, they write because they have something important to say. When you travel to London, take a break from the crown jewels, the changing of the guard, and the rest of the tourist routine, and go to Hyde Park and linger in "Speaker's Corner," the portion of the park reserved for anyone with vocal cords and tenacity. There you will find rationalists and racists, mathematicians and madmen, democrats and demagogues. However objectionable their rhetoric, each speaker has a place to espouse a point of view, and each view is subject to instantaneous rebuke or approval. I am alarmed by racist views expressed in public, but relieved when people of good will challenge the speaker and ridicule his views. Better that such views are expressed in Hyde Park on Sunday morning than in secret meetings on Monday evening.

I detest racism with every fiber of my being, and I know that tracts such as the *Protocols of the Elders of Zion* and *Mein Kampf* are available to the inquisitive reader on Amazon.com at this moment. Only slightly more subtle are the ubiquitous writings that associate skin color with educational and economic destiny.

Whether these articles are penned by authors wearing white sheets or academic robes, the voices of reason must respond. Imagine that you took your children to the park for a few hours of weekend reverie, and just as the kids were finding their favorite playground activity, a bully knocked one child off the teeter-totter and pushed another off a swing. Would you sit there and think, "Gee, even bullies have First Amendment rights"? Or would you confront the bully directly, personally, and publicly? The impulse to write on the subjects about which you are passionate is similar—a visceral autonomic response, a reflection of compulsion rather than the product of a decision. Of course, not every product of your pen or word processor will be so filled with passion, but the impulse behind even the most pedestrian writing must be your personal and professional need to share your views and thus to stake the claim that you have something of importance to say.

Reading to Write

Your passion will be fueled not only by your work, but also by the ideas, research, and experiences of others. Great consultants are voracious readers, consuming a wide variety of professional literature, contemporary journalism, and pleasure reading. Because you make your living communicating complex ideas to a variety of people, the broader your understanding of the field and the deeper your acquaintance with different ways of expressing ideas, the more likely it is that your efforts to communicate will be effective. Some clients will best receive and understand your message when you support it with classic and contemporary research in your field. Thus, your ability to cite (from memory) current research from a variety of sources will be essential to building your credibility. Other clients will better understand a message that is associated with strong imagery and emotion. Thus, your ability to use analogies, literary images, poetry, and a variety of musical and artistic metaphors will serve you well. Other clients will receive your message best when it is linked to contemporary events, and thus your deep understanding of global and domestic issues will help you to communicate your ideas. The amount of reading necessary to communicate with a wide variety of clients can be overwhelming, but here are some ideas to make the task easier:

1. Develop a discipline of always having standby reading, particularly when waiting. Whether it's a ten-minute wait in the line at the grocery store, a 30-minute wait for a solitary dinner on the road, an hour-long wait for airport security, or a two-hour delay during a traffic jam, always have reading material with you. I read hundreds of pages of newspapers, journals, and books every week while others around me are angrily grousing about the inconvenience of their delay.

2. Find research digests and syntheses. No one can possibly read every important article in a field, but it is reasonable for clients and colleagues to assume that you are acquainted with surveys of contemporary work. For example, in educational research, the *Marshall Memo* (www.MarshallMemo.com) provides a five- or six-page summary of articles from more than a score of journals every week. In the business technology arena, there is TechWeb (http://www.techweb.com/newsletters/); for financial information, Bloomberg.com; and for up-to-date news, there are the major online newsweekly sites (money.cnn.com and www.forbes.com, to name just two).

3. Subscribe to a books-on-tape service such as Audible.com. For about $22.00 a month, you get two unabridged audio books or subscriptions to a variety of newspapers, magazines, and journals—and a tiny MP3 player about the size of a pack of chewing gum, but with storage capacity for several audio books. Think you don't have time to read *Harvard Business Review* every month? Do you believe that you'll have to be retired before you can read a biography, novel, or book of short stories for pleasure? With Audible.com, you can have every article at your disposal and "read" it while on the treadmill, in the car, or standing in line.

4. Develop a network of three or four colleagues with whom you share research and contemporary reading. If each of you agrees to read just one journal and summarize the results for the others, you will quadruple your coverage of relevant literature for a very small investment of time. Moreover, forcing yourself to write brief summaries of what you read will help you capture the essence of the articles and force you to communicate in a clear, concise, and understandable manner.

5. Create your own informal data bank of research. I keep "virtual index cards" with direct quotations for articles and books. This is a single word-processing file, with each quotation preceded by a few words that capture the essence of the passage I am quoting. I write the full bibliographic citation down once so that if, many months or years later, I wish to use the quotation in an article or book, I don't have to track down the actual article or book. For me, the simple word-processing file is very handy, more so than a more sophisticated database would be. I use the "find" feature of my word processor to quickly scan the entire file for a term, author, or title and can typically find research within seconds.

This chapter has been concerned with passion, the raw energy that is essential to sustain your career and your personal motivation. Nevertheless, passion alone will not be sufficient if you do not make your consulting enterprise a business success. Therefore, we must now move from the sublime to the practical—how to take your passion, energy, and ideas and translate them into a profitable business.

Service: The Business of Consulting

Passion and Business

Cash Flow

Better Free than Cheap:
Dealing with Client Demands for Discounts

The Crowding-Out Phenomenon:
Helping Clients Allocate Resources

Getting Paid: In Full and On Time

Handling Disagreements

Because consulting is, above all, a service, some consultants are uncomfortable talking about the business details. This reluctance particularly afflicts those in the nonprofit sector, who genuinely believe that the value of their service is not related to price, and that those who need their services the most may be the least able to pay.

I have seen the same uneasiness with business discussions affect attorneys, accountants, and consultants in many fields. Frankly, I don't enjoy these details either, but I have learned this: If you believe deeply in the value of what you do and you are committed to bringing your services to more people, including those who need you the most, then you must pay attention to the business of consulting. Paying attention to business does not mean that you are greedy or mercenary. On the contrary, if you heed the advice in this chapter, you will be able to achieve the financial security necessary to engage in charitable work, provide services for free when appropriate, and reconcile your personal values with your practical financial needs and those of your family and your colleagues.

Passion and Business

How can we reconcile the compelling need for passion described in the previous chapter with the absolute necessity of survival as a business? The late Mark Olson, a good friend who did some of his best writing during the final days of his life, described three enterprises (Olson, 1992). All three organizations had good and committed people, guided by a vision and faith that they were doing the right thing. In the first, the "Feel Good Community Church," they traded away passion for business success, and became more like a country club than a service organization. The next group embraced passion to the point that they failed to survive as an organization. All the passion in the world was of little use when services could not be delivered. The "Glimpse of God," in Olson's terminology, occurred only when leadership was guided by passion without being blinded by it. Though he did not use the term *business,* Olson certainly understood that there are pedestrian elements to organizational survival. For-profit and nonprofit organizations, solo consultants and global enterprises, service and manufacturing enterprises all have basic survival needs in common. Here are just a few of them:

- You need more cash coming in than going out.
- You need completely reliable suppliers of everything from stationery to airline tickets, so that you meet every commitment you make.
- You need colleagues, employees, vendors, and other partners who share your commitment to quality, timeliness, and meeting obligations.
- You need to be able to survive financially without taking a single dollar out of the business for 18 to 24 months.

Cash Flow

A business needs more cash coming in than going out. That's right: surviving organizations need not only revenue, which appears on a financial statement as soon as an invoice is issued, but also real cash—money in the bank. The distinction between cash and revenue is important, as it is possible for an apparently successful organization to sell itself right out of business. Say you accept an order for $5,000 in goods and services on January 1, and you promptly deliver on the contract just one month later, on February 1; you issue an invoice that day and receive full payment on March 1. Even in this best of all possible worlds, there is an interval of at least 60 days between the time you incur costs (electricity, communication, technology, paper, travel, publications, and other components of the services and goods you deliver) and the time you get paid. If you believe passionately in what you do—and you must in order to sustain yourself and your organization—then you must survive financially. In the best sense of the phrase, you run the organization like a business, because whatever the mission and whatever the organization, you must survive if you are to pursue your passion. Business considerations are not antithetical to passion; business principles, such as the cash-flow considerations discussed in this chapter, are the foundation for extending your passion from theory into practice.

Figure 5.1 illustrates the cumulative impact of this lag in cash. This chart shows data that a growing consulting company might appreciate, starting with $5,000 in orders every month, and growing slightly every month. Clients pay right on time, 30 days after they are invoiced. Despite exceptional efforts to collect funds in a timely manner, my organization nevertheless experiences a few clients who take 60, 90, or even 180 days to pay what they owe us. Whether the interval is 60 days, as illustrated in Figure 5.1, or 180 days or longer, the organization will need to have enough available cash to continue operations. Otherwise, despite its apparent success, incoming orders, and popularity with clients and customers, it will fail.

In this simplified example, your organization achieves orders of $5,000 per month, with an annual growth rate of 10 percent. This is not a terrific growth rate—it will take you almost two years to get to $6,000 per month—but it seems reasonable for your enterprise. You are a careful planner and flawless implementer, so you always manage to keep your expenses to 90 percent of your revenues, thus providing a 10 percent return on every engagement. Best of all, your clients always pay on time; there is not a single bad debt or slow-paying client in this example. Everything is working perfectly, but for the first two years of your consulting business,

Figure 5.1		Cash-Flow Realities in a Successful and Growing Business			
Month #	Order Received (10% annual growth)	Expenses to Create Order (10% annual growth rate)	Cash Received	Cash Deficit	Cumulative Deficit
1	$5,000	$4,500		$(4,500)	$(4,500)
2	$5,042	$4,538		$(4,538)	$(9,038)
3	$5,084	$4,575	$5,000	$425	$(8,613)
4	$5,126	$4,614	$5,042	$428	$(8,185)
5	$5,169	$4,652	$5,084	$432	$(7,753)
6	$5,212	$4,691	$5,126	$435	$(7,317)
7	$5,255	$4,730	$5,169	$439	$(6,878)
8	$5,299	$4,769	$5,212	$443	$(6,436)
9	$5,343	$4,809	$5,255	$446	$(5,989)
10	$5,388	$4,849	$5,299	$450	$(5,539)
11	$5,433	$4,889	$5,343	$454	$(5,085)
12	$5,478	$4,930	$5,388	$458	$(4,628)
13	$5,524	$4,972	$5,433	$461	$(4,166)
14	$5,570	$5,013	$5,478	$465	$(3,701)
15	$5,616	$5,055	$5,524	$469	$(3,232)
16	$5,663	$5,097	$5,570	$473	$(2,759)
17	$5,710	$5,139	$5,616	$477	$(2,282)
18	$5,758	$5,182	$5,663	$481	$(1,801)
19	$5,806	$5,225	$5,710	$485	$(1,316)
20	$5,854	$5,269	$5,758	$489	$ (827)
21	$5,903	$5,313	$5,806	$493	$ (334)
22	$5,952	$5,357	$5,854	$497	$ 164
23	$6,002	$5,402	$5,903	$501	$ 665
24	$6,052	$5,446	$5,952	$506	$ 1,170

you are dead broke, spending every dollar of the cash that does come in to pay for work previously done and work in process. Almost two years must elapse before the cash flow is sufficient to allow you to start enjoying the fruit of your labors.

Furthermore, in the example in Figure 5.1, we assumed that the only thing that gave rise to expenses were the orders from clients. What about expenses that you incur without any orders? Each time you travel to a convention or trade show, each time you advertise, each time you update your Web site, you are adding to the expense column without adding any revenues. There are many computer-generated business models that will allow you to generate not only financial statements, but also the all-important cash-flow diagram. Whether your enterprise brings in thousands or millions, you must watch the cash.

If you stop putting money back into the company, it will not grow and you will not be able to fulfill customer orders. If you borrow money, your earnings will be reduced because now you will be paying interest expenses, in addition to your other expenses. If you bring in partners who invest in your business, you will be sharing the profits with other people and thus have a far lower yield for your efforts. Many people who start new entities of any sort—profit-making consultancies or non-profit human services organizations—fail to grasp the principles of cash flow. Because expenses happen before income, even in the most successful organizations, principles of cash flow require that you have excellent and almost unlimited access to borrowed funds, or that you start your organization with substantial savings that are held in reserve and not spent on furniture and computers, and that you reinvest a significant portion of your earnings back into the business so that your organization can continue to expand, rather than rewarding yourself with a nicer car or home.

For most consultants starting out, these facts of life mean that you have already saved enough money to live on for one or two years and that you do not take money out of the business. During my company's first year, I took nothing out and lived on the proceeds of part-time jobs. I taught school, provided free and low-cost test-prep courses, wrote articles for airline magazines (among my very worst literary efforts), and lived in an apartment where, in return for reduced rent, I shoveled snow and mowed the lawn. During the second year, I took out exactly $2,000 per month. Our growth has been strong and, by most measurements, we have become a successful organization, serving clients well, providing great benefits to our employees, and earning fair returns for our employee-owners. We are debt-free and have accumulated a substantial financial reserve. An important part of what makes that entire system work was that we built up the company without taking large amounts of funds out of it.

During the early years of entrepreneurial success, the greatest dangers are material seduction. After all, we're growing, clients love us, orders are coming in—can't I get a new car? How about a bigger office? I didn't know copy machines cost more than $4,000, but hey, we're in the big time now, so let's go for it. The simplified chart in Figure 5.1 assumes that expenses grow in proportion to income. In many cases, however, expenses grow faster than income, because it is easy to assume that we need new employees, equipment, and personal perquisites in anticipation of ever-growing income. When we fall into this trap, the cash-flow deficits can be much worse than are portrayed in the chart.

The challenges of cash flow become compounded when, just as expenses are rising, clients demand discounts, decide to spread their resources around to competitors, pay late, or precipitate conflicts with you about the amount due or the delivery of services and goods you have provided. The balance of this chapter addresses these delicate and very important issues.

Better Free than Cheap: Dealing with Client Demands for Discounts

From the beginning of your consulting career, you will almost certainly face client requests—even demands—for discounts. If your clients are in the corporate world, they will claim to be on a tight budget. If your clients are in the governmental sector or nonprofit world, they will claim that their status entitles them to a discount. I have always found it interesting that the same governmental and nonprofit organizations do not consider demanding discounts from the electric company, telephone company, or the providers of their office supplies and technology needs, but can be insistent and even indignant about demanding discounts from providers of services. You will be well served if you establish a policy for discounted services early in your career.

I learned my lesson in this touchy field at a very early stage. I had routinely provided discounts, under the theory that it was better to do work at a discount than to do no work at all. (When you are starting, no work at all seems to be the pervasive alternative.) However, as my business grew, I was in the unenviable position of being forced to turn down work that would have paid my full rate because I had already committed my time to other clients at a discount. Moreover, what started out as an ethically decent thing to do—granting discounts to those who were pleading poverty—soon became an ethical quagmire. The result was the opposite of my intentions. Some clients that were more demanding than deserving received discounts, whereas others whose budgets were equally tight were willing to respect the value of my services and pay the appropriate price, perhaps cutting elsewhere in the budget or raising revenues. These clients believed that the laborer was worthy of his wages. I suspect that they also paid the telephone repair person, trash hauler, and plumber their full rates—not because any of us were particularly extraordinary, but rather because the client recognized the value of our work. In other words, my discount policy did not reward poverty, but only encouraged aggressive bargaining. The crowning moment in my discounting experience arrived when I devoted a day to a client, providing quality, services, and time that were equal to or greater than those of one of my competitors, who was at the same location. I learned in casual conversation that my competitor had refused to give the discount that I had happily offered. Thus, my discount was used not to help the client, but only to take money out of my pocket and place it in his.

That is when I developed the "better free than cheap" rule. Under this rule, I am committed to providing free services several times every year. I do this not only because I have an ethical obligation to provide free services and share my time and talent, but also because it allows me, with a clear conscience, to refuse to provide discounts. On average, I take approximately 12 completely free (or expenses-only) engagements every year, out of a total of about 90 engagements. This system may not be perfect, but it embodies a commitment to consistent and fair practice that works for me. Moreover, it prevents the inevitable problem of granting discounts on an inconsistent and irregular basis. The world of clients is like a small town, in which one inevitably talks to the other about the most confidential and sensitive matters, including the fees they pay to consultants. Once you give a discount to one, the knowledge of that fact will spread like the gossip in the rabbi's tale, flying through the air like feathers from a shaken pillow. This is a law of the universe: Your discount policy will never remain confidential.

The commitment to providing free services on a regular basis can be exceptionally liberating. This is particularly true when you hold the line very firmly on the value of your services. For example, if your services are worth $5,000 and you provide them for free, you gain far more in the way of good will and future relationships than if you discounted those services to $500. Moreover, when other people who have paid you the $5,000 that you charge hear about a discount, they feel cheated. If the same people hear that you donated services to a worthy cause, they will help the recipients of that donation understand the significant value of your generosity.

You can strategically allocate your free presentations to those areas where you will have the greatest impact or simply the most fun. I have given free time to local libraries and community centers simply because the other presenters were so enchanting that I felt lucky to be on the same stage with them. There was no strategic impact for my company, but it was a sheer joy to spend time this way and these institutions could never have afforded to pay the going rate of any of the speakers they had lined up for their events. However, these organizations did provide a participative audience, a compelling subject, and a group of engaging presenters. Everyone walked away from the event knowing that value is not a function of price.

At other times, I have provided free or expense-only services to organizations to which I have a deep personal and philosophical commitment. In other cases, free services are offered for strategic business reasons—where I have the opportunity for national or international exposure in a way that will help not only me but all of my colleagues as well. Although I do my very best in all presentations, it is fair to say that a presentation to a local group does not have the same long-term impact as does a presentation to a national or international group. When I allocate my free engagements, I try to consider all these factors—strategic advantages for my colleagues and me, personal and philosophical interest, or simply a great deal of fun. Nobody would confuse these efforts with Mother Teresa's, but my policies do represent one way of dealing in an ethical manner with the issue of discounting.

The gray area of "honoraria" can create issues that are better avoided. It is essential that you be consistent, because what one person calls an honorarium another will see as a consulting fee in academic disguise. In my experience, the term *honorarium* is used as a euphemism for discount. Because you are an ethical professional, the quality of your work will not vary depending on the amount or label of the fee. Every engagement deserves your very best efforts. When IBM sells a computer to a university, the corporation does not receive an honorarium for its products. The company provides a series of services and products, and receives a market price for them. Similarly, if you are offered an honorarium in lieu of your regular fee, it is better to live by the "better free than cheap" rule and donate that honorarium to a scholarship fund or other worthy cause than to accept it and have it misinterpreted as a discounted fee.

The hard line on discounting does not imply that you cannot be creative about the way in which you structure fees. For example, many clients' purchasing rules establish inconsistent budgets for each category of expenses. Let's say the value of your consulting services is $20,000—but the client is permitted to pay only $2,000 for that particular category. That same client may also be able to invest $50,000 in technology and permanent resources such as CD-ROMs, DVDs, and publications. Successful consultants have books, CD-ROMs, DVDs, or other materials that clients can purchase, so you can work out a package that meets the client's budget and your fee requirements. As long as you are treated fairly, and in turn treat all your clients in a comparable manner, you can ethically accept a lower fee provided that you are simultaneously providing other valuable resources to the client at an appropriate price. The same phenomenon may be associated with client fiscal years: sometimes it is necessary to provide services in one year and delay payment to a future year, as that is the only timing that is consistent with the client's funding. This flexibility is simply part of the provision of exceptional service, and does not compromise the integrity of the no-discount rule.

Two final words on discounting. First, you can expect to be confronted with the contention that "everybody else does it." When I was 15 years old, I worked in a shoe store. Thinking that I was doing the right thing, I unloaded the trucks, stocked the shelves, and, in my spare time, straightened up the displays, including the discount tables. The manager, wise in the impulses of bargain-hunting shoppers, admonished me and ran his hands through my neatly displayed discount table. "People want to work for bargains," he explained. The bargains that the customers were to find were as illusory as the messy display. The layers of stickers on discounted shoes told the tale: The bottom sticker, which no one but the most persistent label peeler would see, showed the original price of $19.99. The next sticker displayed the original discount of $17.99. The third and final sticker showed $24.99, with a hand-drawn line through it and a scrawl that said "20% off." You do the math. This is not a discount, but clever marketing. When a client recently claimed that a competitor, notorious for overpriced blarney, had offered a "60 percent discount," I knew that this was a trick or illusion, based only on inflation of the price before the granting of the discount.

The second and last word on discounting is one that clients rarely consider. Where do discounted dollars come from—the discount fairy? I have asked clients who demanded a discount this question: "Who do you want me to pay less? What bill do you want me not to pay? Which computer or telephone should I disconnect?" Their response, after a long pause, has been, "I never thought of it that way." In consulting, this is a particularly difficult issue. If you are manufacturing things, such as books or videos, there is a certain economy of scale, and it makes sense to give a discount on an order of 1,000 units compared to 100 units. But, as Abraham Lincoln said of a lawyer's time, the hours in the day are the consultant's stock in trade. Once an hour is spent, it cannot be replaced. If you choose to discount your services, you will either pay yourself less or pay your colleagues less. The chances that your discount will help your client or enhance your reputation are outweighed by the probability that your discount will enrich your competitors and persuade all those who hear about it that you are cheaper than you claim to be.

The Crowding-Out Phenomenon: Helping Clients Allocate Resources

Budgets are a zero-sum game. In other words, one dollar provided to vendor A is a dollar that cannot also be spent on vendor B. In some cases, this presents a moral dilemma: shall we devote funds to food for starving children, prescription drugs for the ailing elderly, or training programs to help unemployed workers gain an opportunity in the world of work? In such dilemmas, let the wisdom of Solomon prevail. In your case, though, the choices are more mundane. Will the client spend limited resources on you, or on your competitor? Or, in an attempt to be politically correct, will the client split the difference and allow you and your competitor both to attempt to do half-complete jobs?

If you embraced the message of passion in the previous chapter, you know the right thing to do. You compete to the end, demanding that the client allocate disproportionate resources to your efforts. You do this knowing that every dollar devoted to your contract will be taken from your competitor, and you do not suffer a moment's guilt about it. In fact, you know that this "crowding-out" effect is essential to your client's success. I have worked in schools, for example, that have run seven simultaneous reading programs, all competing for limited time and the attention of students and teachers. Everyone involved would have been better served had the salesperson for just one of those programs been sufficiently aggressive to demand and achieve a larger contract, so that the schools had only one or two reading programs that would receive the attention and focus of all students and teachers. Corporations inexplicably purchase multiple programs in customer services, leadership, and time management, each of which is inconsistent with the others. If the best of the lot had demanded a greater share of management's time, money, and focus, the organization would have been much better served.

Figure 5.2	Competition Comparison Chart	
Client Criteria	**Your Unique Strength**	**Your Competitor's Alternative**
1. Quality		
2. Personalized services		
3. Follow-up support		
4. Responsiveness to individual client needs		
5. Other unique capabilities that you offer		

So ask yourself this question: What do you do that is, without any question and beyond a shadow of a doubt, better than what your competitors do? Complete the chart in Figure 5.2, listing on the left-hand side what you do that is unique, extraordinary, and compelling. On the right-hand side, list the pale imitations of your services that your competitors provide. Whenever you are tempted to offer a discount, refer to this chart and remind yourself that each time clients have the discretion to allocate funds, time, and energy, they can choose the left or the right side of the table. If they choose the left, they will be better off. This is not hardball competition, but rather your ethical obligation to the client. By crowding out your competitor, the client is better served. This is not the time to claim that "we can all get along"; instead, it is the time to say that every stakeholder your client must serve is better off when the client makes the choice to embrace one alternative and reject another.

Getting Paid: In Full and On Time

Bobby Fischer, the world chess champion, was famous for many things, but beyond his brilliance on the chessboard, I recall his habit of walking into a tournament and, before the first pawn was moved, asking, "Do you have my check?" I've seen nationally known consultants do the same. When my 90-day receivables exceeded half a million dollars and theirs were zero, I learned the wisdom of their ways. Though getting paid in advance is rarely possible, it is certainly possible to get paid either on the day services are rendered or within a very few days thereafter. Thanks to collection procedures learned over the years, my company's ratio of 90-day-old receivables to the total has declined to a fraction of its previous level. Moreover, the decline in the age of our accounts receivable is directly related to our current cash balance and our overall financial health. Here are some practical guidelines to getting paid in full and on time.

Get everything in writing. We do not purchase tickets, print handouts, or go to engagements without a written commitment. As this chapter was being written, I received a call from one of our largest clients. "We have a potential problem," she began. "Another consultant claims to have had a verbal agreement to provide services at the same time you are scheduled. But your organization provided written agreements and multiple confirmations, and all we have from the other consultant is a hazy recollection of a telephone call 11 months ago. This is really awkward, but we want to keep our agreement with you because it is so clearly documented, and we'll work out something else with the other consultant." Let me be clear about what the phrase *in writing* means. Yogi Berra was right when he claimed that "a verbal agreement isn't worth the paper it's written on." People laugh at Yogi's malapropisms, then think that they have completed a communication by leaving a voice mail recording, hissing a hasty message during an elevator ride, or dredging up a hazy recollection of an ancient telephone conversation. Professionals confirm things in writing. They don't send emails, faxes, or voice mails, but have written confirmation and acceptance of every detail, from the fee to the engagement dates to the nonsmoking room on the side of the hotel away from the railroad tracks. Professionals do not leave communication to chance.

Get a purchase order number. In many consulting engagements, the person who wants the services is not necessarily the person who actually approves the expenditure of funds for the services. It only took us one time to learn that, after investing thousands of dollars in a project, a completely different department can say, "Sorry, but we never approved that and we're not going to pay for it." In most client organizations, there are only two ways of authorizing expenditures: writing a check or issuing a purchase order for automatic approval of a check in the future. Do not put you, your colleagues, or your organization at risk without either a check or a purchase order.

Confirm client expectations. In my company, we have learned to put agendas in the contract. If we think a full day extends from 7:00 a.m. through 3:00 p.m., but the client thinks that the same full day runs from 9:00 a.m. through 5:00 p.m., there will inevitably be hard feelings, missed airplane flights, and worst of all, missed client engagements on the following day. Confirm the details of the agenda well in advance and in writing. If you conduct a national or global business, these details are exceptionally important. When I work on the west coast on Tuesday and have an obligation on the east coast on Wednesday, I must depart the west coast at about 1:00 p.m., and that means arriving at the airport no later than noon, at the latest. The time to work out the details of these schedule requirements is at the very beginning of the contract for the engagement—not in the weeks preceding delivery of the contracted services.

Become personally involved in collections. I hate dealing with money. As a rule, I won't discuss fees, contracts, or any other element of money with clients. I have very smart and capable business people on my team who are happy to do this. However, if there is a problem with payment—and that means anything overdue by 90 days or more—then I become personally involved. I review a list of every over-90-day bill each Friday afternoon. In extreme cases, we cancel engagements and refuse to conduct business with organizations that are chronically late in paying their bills. It is no bargain to allow a client (even a repeat client) to create artificially high revenues that, in the end, generate only the illusion of revenue and the actuality of costs, and to inflict emotional distress on your colleagues and you because that client is a deadbeat. As unpleasant as it is, you must be willing to make the call that says, "I very much value our relationship, but in order to continue it, I need to have a check from you tomorrow." And then you follow through, either getting the money or terminating the relationship.

Handling Disagreements

Here is a rule to live by: You do not win arguments with clients. If you choose to argue, you can assume that they are no longer your clients. As I wrote in the opening pages to this book, I subscribe to the "wax your car and wash your dog" theory of quality control. If a client is dissatisfied (and in the course of thousands of engagements and millions of miles of travel, it has happened), we never—not ever—offer excuses. We say, "What can we do to make this right? If we didn't meet your expectations, then we will refund your money and provide you a new engagement for free." We add, in an attempt to lighten the mood, an offer to wax their car and wash their dog, assuming that they are more prone to own poodles than pit bulls. We will do anything to make a client happy, and in the very few instances in which the client was dissatisfied, we have done everything humanly possible to make it right.

In most cases, our investment in quality pays off. More than eight years ago, we provided an inadequately prepared speaker for a state superintendents' association meeting. We admitted the mistake, refunded the money, and provided a new presenter for free. Today, that state is one of our largest clients. The month this chapter was written, we had a client who was dissatisfied with a presentation. Within days, one of our senior executives met with the client and accompanied the client to a subsequent engagement. If we are wrong, we react—indeed, overreact—to client demands.

My strong prejudice is that the client is right and we are wrong. When we get low quality ratings (unusual as that is), we can sort through thousands of data elements and find the following underlying causes:

- *Poor pre-engagement work.* When clients claim that we didn't meet their expectations, the plain fact is that we failed to learn what those expectations were. We can't learn about client expectations if we fail to conduct a comprehensive and detailed pre-engagement conference. The first chapter and Appendix A provided advice and help on this point. Ignore it at your peril.

- *Canned presentations.* All our clients know that they are unique. Although they might have admired a presentation they saw elsewhere, they are far more satisfied with one that reflects a consideration of their personal and peculiar circumstances. Our practice is to review the client's Web site and interview

its key people. Even when we use standard handouts, we add new Power-
Point slides to reflect the local context and address the client's unique circumstances and needs.

- ■ *Elevation of national data over local data.* As a researcher and writer, I can
  be too easily seduced by my own statistics. My greatest failures have occurred
  when I believed my own press. A more appropriate reaction is to distrust
  adulation and consider criticism. Clients are best served by action research
  conducted by their own colleagues, and consultants should be the source of
  methodology supporting local action research.

In general, my support of clients at the expense of consultants
will prevail, presuming client good will and assuming our own failings. But there are
times—limited and very rare—when we have been sandbagged. The client was wrong,
and we were right. Though we do not say it publicly, there are exceedingly rare times
when the time-honored phrase "The customer is always right" is false. We have done
business in 50 states and five continents. Our database contains more than 40,000 individual contacts and we undertake more than a thousand client engagements each year.
With that volume of business, there will inevitably be a few times (however rare) when
we provide precisely what a client asked for but the client remains dissatisfied. In these
cases, we do not fight, but withdraw from the fight. It's a big world out there, and your
emotional, financial, and physical energy will be better invested in supporting your colleagues and intellectual champions rather than fighting those with whom you disagree.

We now move from the sublime to the ridiculous—the glam-
orous world of travel. Unless you are lucky enough to have a consulting business that
will grow within the limits of your local road network, or you are willing to travel on
a mass transit network, you will be forced to walk through metal detectors that regard
your collar stays as lethal weapons and consider your extra supply of triple-A batteries
for your dictation machine as particularly suspicious. There will be hotel receptionists
who ask for your photographic identification, despite their having seen your craggy
face at 2:00 a.m. multiple times in the past three months. There will be cab drivers
whose principal objective is to ask you to help them learn enough English to pass their
next employment exam. There will be hotels where you will be unable to sleep without
narcotic assistance, because of the noise generated by the passion in adjacent bedrooms,
the stomps on the treadmill in the adjacent exercise room, the clangs of the adjacent
construction area, or the rattles of the adjacent railroad tracks. When clients put you
in these rooms because the venue is "historic" or "natural" or even "convenient," you
will need to consider the advantages of the less historic motel that is 20 miles away.
In the next chapter, we'll consider the practical elements of successful travel for working consultants.

CHAPTER 6

Logistics: The Glamorous World of Travel, and Other Myths

Travel

Time

Commitments

Giving Clients Your Very Best

If Leonardo da Vinci were providing consulting services to the art world, he could be undone by poor logistics. No matter how brilliant your ideas and how superior your service, if you do not attend to the logistics of an engagement, you can be the da Vinci of the consulting world and still fall flat on your face if you do not attend to the details we will discuss in this chapter.

There are times when every detail of an engagement is flawless. The drive to the airport is without incident and the security line is short. The boarding process is smooth as silk and the person sitting next to you neither spills a cup of coffee on your freshly cleaned suit nor falls asleep with an arm, neck, mouth-breathing noise, or flatulence intruding into your personal space. The taxi queue is short and the driver knows, without asking for directions, the most direct route to your hotel. Room service is still available, and you are able to get a salad and cup of soup for less than $30. After dinner, you find that the Internet works the first time and with a minimum of effort, and the next day's wakeup call is precisely synchronized with the alarm that you set just in case. The exercise room is open at 5:30 a.m. and there are more treadmills than runners, as well as clean towels and fresh water. There is hot water in the shower and you can distinguish the shampoo from the conditioner without using a magnifying glass. Your host greets you in the lobby and you arrive at the engagement an hour early, finding the room arranged precisely as you had requested, with every technology need met. The audience arrives well informed, prepared, and enthusiastic, and their creature comforts—food, room temperature, and decent chairs—have been attended to with the same care that has made the entire experience perfect for you. The cell-phone detectors at the door automatically disconnected or destroyed every one of those plague-ridden devices as participants entered the room. You were introduced by someone who spoke as if she knew you and had a personal interest in what you had to say. We have not even considered what you say or do; this paragraph has simply described a few of the logistical details that contribute to the success or failure of every client engagement.

Then there are the other times—and all of these things have happened to me. For many years, I arranged all of these details myself. Today, I have a wonderful colleague, Cathy Shulkin, who helps arrange and triple-check every logistical arrangement. Nevertheless, things happen. Flights are delayed and canceled, forcing me to drive all night and arrive, sleepless, exhausted, and unfocused, but at least on time, to my engagement. I have missed only one engagement in my career, but I've driven all night and chartered cars and aircraft in order to make a commitment. Luggage is lost, leaving me to buy a suit at 8:45 p.m. at a Men's Wearhouse that closed at 9:00 p.m. Though I remain a loyal customer of that store, I learned from that experience never to check luggage on the road. Though I have sat next to some charming people, including the late Ray Charles and the very witty Ben Stein, I have also endured some seatmates so offensive that I have either moved or devoted a good deal of the trip to the confines of the lavatory. Room service is most frequently closed when I arrive after midnight at a hotel, and Internet connections continue to be inconsistent, poorly supported, and overpriced. Exercise rooms that are adequately equipped are rare, and many of them are dangerous. My ride is late or missing. The facilities are laughably inadequate. In the past few months, hotel staffs have set up tables directly in front of posts, making it impossible to see the presenter; events have been scheduled in high school gymnasiums where participants are expected to sit for hours without back support or any surface on which to write notes; rooms have been uncomfortably hot or cold, making climate control as elusive indoors as outdoors. People arrive at meetings saying, "I don't know why I'm here—I was just told to show up" and they are angry, disengaged, and rude. Not only do cell phones ring, but people also take the calls and conduct loud conversations—most recently in the front row of an auditorium holding more than 1,000 people. The public address system does not work, the projectors are missing or incompatible with my computer, and the small screens were designed for 30 people rather than the 300 that are attempting to see them. It doesn't make any difference how brilliant my presentation is—these logistical matters almost completely undermine and obscure the message. In the next few pages are some rules I have learned about the logistical elements of consulting.

Travel

The following "Reeves Rules for Travel" are simply suggestions, unless you happen to be a colleague of mine or are simply someone interested in reducing stress during the distinctly unglamorous part of your consulting career that involves travel. In those instances, forget the gentle suggestive tone—these are rules, mandates, and survival requirements. My experiences are not universally perfect, but for someone who has traveled more than two million miles in the past ten years and continues to put on about a quarter-million miles every year, these recommendations are the distillation of hard-won lessons.

1. *Treat people in the travel industry with courtesy and respect.* There is very little evidence that any plane ever flew faster, any weather pattern changed, or any hotel accommodation ever improved because a customer was rude to a flight attendant, yelled at a gate agent, or attempted to intimidate a desk clerk. Though courtesy and respect may seem alien in the world of the harried traveler, they still go a long way toward getting you what you want. There will be times when you are given an upgrade not because you had the certificates in the account, but simply because you said "please" and "thank you" and treated the counter employee like a fellow member of the human race. You are let into the exercise facility two hours before it officially opens because the desk clerk remembers that when you checked in the night before, you wished him a good night. You are given a rental car when everyone else is told that they are sold out, and you are given a nonsmoking suite when there is a long line of people being diverted to other hotels: in neither case were you more

deserving of service than other people, but you were the only one in line who did not resort to anger and intimidation to get your way.

What if I'm wrong about this? Surely you have observed a few cases in which the bully got his way while the mild-mannered, polite chump received only disrespect. Surely this may happen, but the rewards of civility far outweigh those of boorish behavior. And even when the bad guys win a few rounds, you will still go to bed knowing that you were a kind and decent human being. That's worth a good night's sleep that bullies rarely get.

2. *Select a primary air carrier, hotel chain, rental car company, and livery service and be dog-loyal to them.* I have found that loyalty is returned in ways that are unexpectedly helpful. These are not simply the frequent flier miles and occasional upgrades—everybody does that. These are the times when the security line is two hours long and you are escorted to the front of the line in time to make your flight. These are the times when, without your having to ask, you are re-routed around a city beset by bad weather. You will be escorted to your newly arranged flight when everyone else is standing in line to make arrangements for the next day. You talk to a real person when everyone else is frantically entering numbers or shouting at a maddening voice-recognition system. You will get a room on the concierge floor rather than the one next to a college frat party and you will get a decent breakfast without standing in line at the restaurant. When your primary airline and hotel make a mistake—and they will—they will be very sorry, refunding your money and ensuring that you are satisfied. These things really happen to me, not only because I am a very good customer, but because even when things go wrong, I remember Rule No. 1.

3. *Never check luggage.* I make more than 100 take-offs, and (I hope) an equal number of landings each year. Each of those departures will take 15 minutes longer, and the arrivals 30 to 45 minutes longer, if I have to check luggage. By packing efficiently—and I can get seven days' worth of clothes into a single carry-on piece of luggage—I save 150 to 200 hours a year. I travel in the suit I will wear to my meetings, packing only shirts, socks, underwear, and workout clothes. I can iron a wrinkled jacket and pants far more easily than I can carry another suit in a checked bag, and the chances are that anything in a checked bag will require ironing anyway. Airlines are increasingly using smaller airplanes and, as a result, even approved carry-on luggage does not always fit in the cabin. Nevertheless, checking bags at the side of the plane and picking them up immediately after you land, right next to the plane, is vastly preferable to checking luggage and waiting for the bags to be delivered to the baggage claim area. The same Mark Olson whose insights highlighted the previous chapter used to advise his friends to "travel light," a concept which for Mark had multiple meanings (Olson, 2002). There is something enormously liberating about

downsizing suitcases, briefcases, and even the contents of one's pockets and wallet. A good deal of this downsizing is possible because of technology and miniaturization, but despite the fact that one can carry the *Encyclopedia Britannica* on microchips that are a fraction of the size of a cell phone, people seem to be carrying more with them with each succeeding year. These days I endeavor to start light and get lighter, bringing with me newspapers, journals, and magazines that will be discarded or left for the next curious passenger during each segment of a trip. When I am given gifts or oversized documents while traveling, I accept them graciously and arrange for them to be shipped to my home. When I can do so graciously, I accept the gift, offer profuse and personal thanks (including, without fail, a personal thank-you note), and then give the assortment of meat, cheese, candy, and other goodies to hotel staff members who will genuinely appreciate it. When I noticed that my multi-decade accumulation of T-shirts was getting out of control, I started bringing the worst of the lot with me on trips, simply discarding them after morning exercise. This allows me to travel much lighter, makes the job of the inspector who must go through my laundry much less unpleasant, and allows me to buy new T-shirts celebrating the Red Sox with much less guilt.

4. Don't argue with security personnel. This is a bad strategy in Frankfurt, where the security agents hold Uzi machine guns, and it is equally bad in American airports, where the Transportation Security Agency employees are equipped principally with the unfettered right to make you miss a flight if they are sufficiently dilatory in their tasks. Let me speak to you as the person right behind you in line. If the TSA lady asks you to take off your shoes, then take off the blasted shoes! If she asks you to remove your belt, watch, bracelet, or necklace, please do not engage in any discourse about the metal content or about how the TSA officials at other airports had different requirements; just do as you are asked. If they explain to you that the scissors, nail file, knife, and corkscrew that no one else had detected in your past five flights will be confiscated, the only appropriate response is, "Thank you for doing such a careful job." If you are selected for supplemental screening and you are mortified as the most private possessions in your suitcase are displayed for the world to see, don't complain; simply forget the rule about not checking luggage and be prepared to give up a few hundred hours of your life in order to preserve your modesty.

5. Systematically reduce the time you spend waiting in lines. That may sound silly given the interminable lines at airports these days, but there are practical things you can do to reduce or even eliminate some lines. Some airlines allow you to print your boarding pass at home using an Internet connection. Almost all airlines now have automated check-in processes that are no more difficult to use than an automated teller at the bank. Some airports—Boston, New York LaGuardia, and Los Angeles are examples that come to mind—have different security lines that lead to the same set of concourses. A few extra steps to the least popular entry point saves a great deal of time.

Be the first or last person onto the airplane. Because I have a fetish about making good use of my time, I like to use every second of it, even when waiting in line. In some lines, I can read, return phone calls, or even write. Unfortunately, the time consumed in boarding an aircraft—sometimes 15 to 20 minutes— is almost always lost to any productive pursuit. If I'm the first to board (a privilege of being a frequent flier), then I can immediately sit down and get to work. If I'm the last to board, then I spent the 20 minutes while everyone else was boarding in the waiting area, reading, writing, or otherwise getting work done. Just as the boarding door is closing, I can walk on, take my seat, and again get back to work.

6. *Invest in ear candy.* You will have happier and more productive trips when you eliminate noise from the outside. Start with inexpensive earplugs. The best are those designed for hunters who must protect their hearing from the noise and shock of their weapons. The best earplugs expand after they are inserted into your ear and provide almost complete silence once they expand. In addition, invest in a set of noise-canceling headphones. (The much-advertised Bose headphones are state of the art, but they are pricey and bulky. A new generation of much smaller headphones is available from many electronics dealers.) Complete the ear candy suite with the tiniest possible digital music player and load it with your favorite music and audio books.

7. *Get a computer that you can actually use for travel.* I am using my third Sony Vaio, about three pounds with built-in wireless connectivity and a DVD player, and it provides more than seven hours of battery life. It's the only laptop I know of that can actually be used on an airplane without lethal consequences should the person sitting in front of you choose to recline the seat. With the rapid changes in technology and the competitive environment, Sony may or may not hold its lead in creating the smallest and best-equipped computers, but your laptop will always be one of your most important investments. Buy a used car and forget the hand-sewn Italian ties—but don't skimp on your laptop. Each year or 18 months, get the lightest, smallest, most powerful machine on the market.

8. *Buy or rent a navigation system.* As with most technology, these get better and cheaper every year. Even if you have to pay $10 a day for a global positioning system through a rental car company, isn't it worth $10 to arrive at the right place and on time? Although these systems contain errors and do not always account for road closures, detours, and new construction, they are nevertheless far superior to most human directions, particularly when you are attempting to read those directions in the dark while traveling on a strange freeway.

9. Politely decline evening social engagements with clients. In some consulting enterprises, evening dinners are required as an essential part of the engagement. Although I attempt to avoid them, I still attend client dinners perhaps two or three times a year, even though I almost always regret having acquiesced to the invitation. Consider the probability that an agreement will be reached or a breakthrough understanding will occur, and compare that to the probability that someone will drink too much, say too much, smoke too much, or consume your time that would otherwise have been devoted to answering email, returning calls, or simply getting to sleep at a reasonable hour in your home time zone. I always am available for breakfast meetings and encourage that with clients. Breakfast meetings tend to be brief, focused, and (unlike evening meetings) fueled by caffeine rather than alcohol.

10. Minimize jet lag. This rule must be separated into two segments—domestic and international work. For domestic travel, I don't change my watch. I always stay on my home time zone, waking and retiring as close to the same time as possible every day. That means that when traveling from Boston to San Francisco, it's three in the morning in California when I bound out of bed—the same time I would if I were in Boston as the radio announced that it was time for the 6:00 a.m. news. When it's 8:00 p.m. in California and a more sociable person might head for a night on the town, my watch reminds me that it's 11:00 p.m. in Boston and time for bed. When I consider how put out most people are by the twice-yearly change to and from Daylight Savings Time, an adjustment of only an hour, I wonder how they would cope with weekly trips across two or three time zones. Indiana farmers have observed that cows care little about Daylight Savings Time and remain on a consistent schedule, obliviously chewing their cuds while clueless humans change the hands on the clock. I aspire to the wisdom of that farmer and the serenity of that cow.

International travel works on a different set of rules, so my best advice is to adapt to the local time as quickly as possible. If you travel all night to Paris and land at 7:00 a.m. local time, be prepared to put in a full day, even as your body attempts to lure you to take a nap. If you succumb to the temptation and nod off for a few hours, you will be wide awake at two in the morning and ready to take a nap during an important meeting during the next day. There are a variety of nonaddictive sleep aids, and most seasoned travelers find their own mix of herbal, pharmaceutical, and other creative remedies to make relatively immediate adjustments to their sleep schedules. If you intend to do a great deal of international travel, then develop some rules that will protect your mental and physical health as well as your relationships.

For a while early in my career, I thought nothing of jetting from Denver to Anchorage to Cairo to London and back—all in a week—and expecting to resume domestic work the day after landing, as if I had just finished a normal work week. Two of my friends who do extensive international work avoid this sort of self-destructive regime by establishing their own rules. One requires a minimum of two weeks (ten paid engagement days) for international work. When the client insists that he is needed for only two days, he explains that he doesn't expect the client to pay for the other eight days, but he does expect the client to arrange engagements for the other eight days—an obligation they almost always fulfill. An acquaintance who does extensive business consulting abroad charges three times his normal rate for international work. Whether the engagement is one day or five, he knows that international travel takes a toll on his body and his family, and this fee schedule allows him to schedule some very deliberate home time before and after international engagements. If he is abroad three days, his firm receives the same revenue as if he had worked domestically for nine days, and he can have preparation and recovery time without an impact on his conscience or bank account. My personal rules are somewhat more modest, requiring a minimum of four days for international engagements and charging only 1.5 times my regular rate.

The key is that you must develop your own rules and stick with them. I have had clients who have, incredibly, suggested that I should do international work for free because, after all, I could include some sightseeing as part of the trip. Sorry: if I want a vacation, my family and I will find a cell-phone-free environment far, far away. If I'm working, I'm working, and however enchanting the local culture may be, I cannot wait to get back home. Your rules certainly need not be my rules, but remember this: Whenever anyone suggests to you that you should work for them for free or for a discounted price, because "it will be fun" or "it will be good for you," many loud alarm bells should go off in your head. When they need someone to repair their computers, provide an immunization, or inspect the plumbing, they never suggest that the labor should be free because the environment is interesting.

Time

If you were a jewelry merchant, how would you react to a prospective customer who said he wanted to "borrow" a diamond, but made it clear to you that it would not be returned? What if she wanted to "try out" an emerald that you would never see again? What if he was sufficiently forthright to say that he was taking your sapphire and never intended to return it—but he would say very good things about your jewelry establishment and that would help you gain more business in the future?

In fact, you are a jewelry merchant. You start every day with 24 diamonds, 1,440 emeralds, and 86,400 sapphires. The diamonds are the hours, the emeralds the minutes, and the sapphires the seconds. You can give them away, sell them, or throw them away, but you cannot save them for another day. Just as the jeweler has an inventory that must be sold or given away, so does the consultant have an inventory of hours, minutes, and seconds that must be used wisely. In the consulting business, your time is your money, so it is as important to track how you invest your time as it is to track how you invest your money. Some people might think I'm a bit obsessive on this point, literally tracking the time it takes me to shower and dress (Figure 6.1), but I do this for a reason. When I say that something is important to me, and then discover that I devoted less time to it than I spent in the shower, those numbers say more about my priorities than my empty words.

Figure 6.1 shows my time allocation for September 2004, and it's not a pretty picture. Though my time devoted to family is better than it was in previous months, I also claim to greatly value community service and music. In both

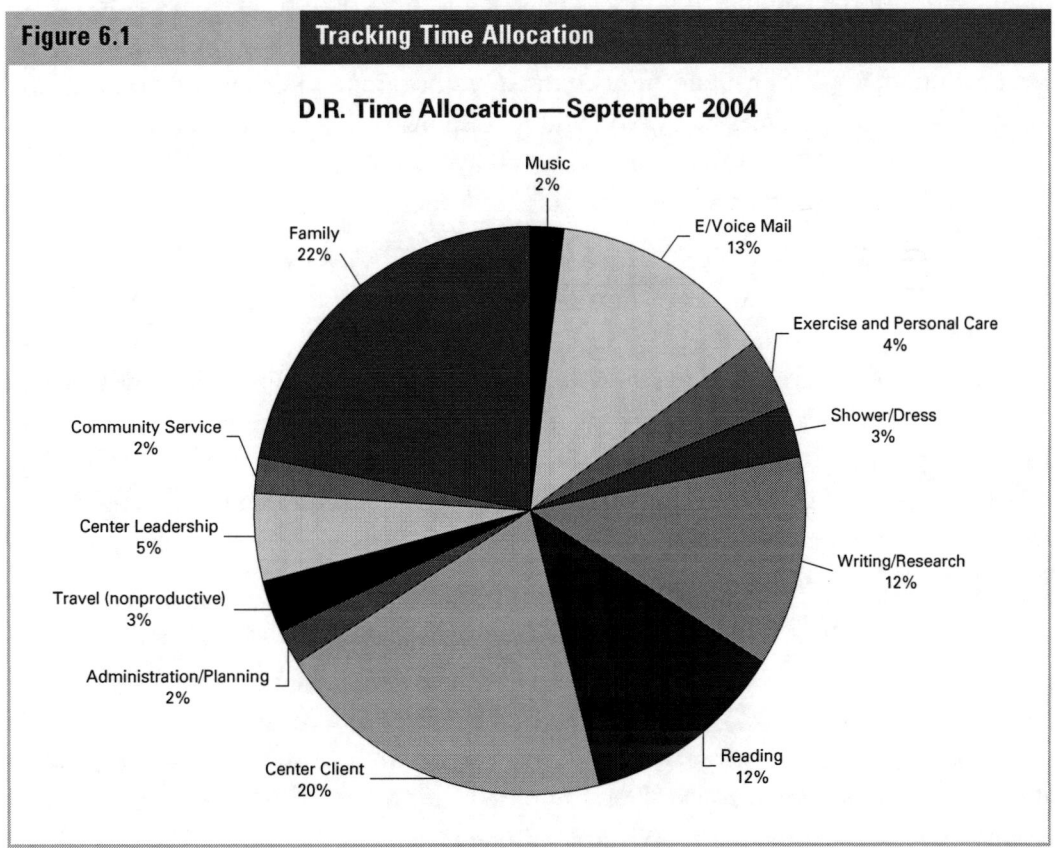

Figure 6.1   **Tracking Time Allocation**

D.R. Time Allocation—September 2004

Music 2%
E/Voice Mail 13%
Family 22%
Exercise and Personal Care 4%
Shower/Dress 3%
Community Service 2%
Center Leadership 5%
Writing/Research 12%
Travel (nonproductive) 3%
Administration/Planning 2%
Reading 12%
Center Client 20%

of those categories, however, the numbers don't lie. Unless I took exceptionally long showers in September (a luxury not possible with two teenagers in the house), the plain fact is that my records of community service and practicing the piano that month were awful. The real culprit is clear: 13 percent of my waking hours for that month were devoted to responding to email and voice mail. Though I attempt to be very diligent about responding to email and voice mail in a timely manner, it's also true that I tend to over-respond, providing multiparagraph explanations when a sentence or two would have sufficed. Worse yet, I sometimes respond to emails that are not even directed to me, but vainly presume that I can add some enlightenment on a subject that was only tangentially my business in the first place.

As a long-term student of time management in general and a relentless advice-giver about the efficient uses of voice mail and email, I'm not proud of this. I share this data to make the point that even the most diligent time managers must be scrupulous about it, comparing our goals to our actual performance, calling ourselves to account when we come up short, and taking steps to improve. For example, the best way to maintain excellent service but reduce the time devoted to voice mail and email is to turn the automated notification systems off. If you react to every "beep" of a new incoming email as if you were Dr. Pavlov's poodle, you will not have five uninterrupted minutes day or night. If, in contrast, you respond to email and voice mail in clusters two or three times a day, you will be responsive yet focused. Your correspondents will almost always receive same-day service, and you will refrain from engaging in the back-and-forth that allows a single email question to explode into a half-hour ping-pong match.

Although time management systems vary widely from one proponent and vendor to another, their essential elements are remarkably similar. Mark McCormick (1984) uses distinctly low-tech legal pads, and the Franklin-Covey system (Smith, 1994) offers a dizzying array of complex forms and computerized organizers, but every effective time management system includes these common components: daily prioritized task list (DPTL), project/task differentiation, personal accountability, and frequent time for reflection and planning.

The DPTL is to the effective time manager what washing hands is to the McDonald's employee. If you value cleanliness, you wash your hands. If *you* value the diamonds, emeralds, and sapphires of your time, then you have a DPTL. You take each word seriously. You update the DPTL daily. Busy consultants have multiple demands on their time, and today's "A" may become tomorrow's "C"—if the update does not take place daily, you will have hundreds of "A" priorities and that effectively means that you might as well have none of them.

The "P" means that your work is prioritized. Here the "Rule of Six" (Reeves, 2002a) applies. If you have more than six "A1" priorities, you are engaging in self-delusion. The DPTL says what few people are willing to say out loud: that some tasks are more important than others. At any given time, I might have more than 100 items on my task list, and I have colleagues who regularly have more than 300 items on theirs. If you were to combine all of your tasks on various forms and systems into one, you might find that your tasks range into the hundreds as well. But if you have more than six "top priorities," *you are kidding yourself.*

The "T" means that you are focused on tasks, not projects. If the line on your notebook says, "Write a book" or "Revise the Human Resources Policies," then you don't have a task, but a project. If instead the line says, "Finish section 6.2 of the book" or "Write the ESOP policy," then it's possible that you have something that is defined with sufficient specificity to be called a *task*.

The "L" means that it's really there, not a figment of your imagination. Excellent time managers, from Benjamin Franklin to Hyrum Smith, either start or end their day with the list. Form C-3 in Appendix C shows an example of a DPTL. You can reproduce it or discard it as a hopeless anachronism. The key is that you use some device, from a piece of paper to a Palm Pilot, to list all your tasks—personal, professional, and volunteer—in a single place and in a prioritized manner. You update it every day. You live by the prioritization, eschewing the call you would like to make for the call you need to make, subordinating the article you would love to write to the article you are committed to write.

Project/Task Differentiation

A major failing of typical time management systems is that they fail to distinguish between projects and tasks. Essentially, *projects* are composed of many smaller tasks. *Tasks* are items that can be completed within a typical segment of your day—usually not longer than 45 minutes to an hour. "Draft overtime policies" is a task, but "Revise human resources policies" is a project. "Revise Chapter 6" is a task, whereas "Write a book" is a project. When a Daily Prioritized Task List is dominated by projects rather than tasks, it becomes discouraging to write the same thing down day after day. The writer feels like a failure and the sheer monotony causes you to let the time management system lapse into disuse. Great time managers of any age—the sixth-grader working on a school project or the senior executive working on an international acquisition or the graduate student completing a dissertation—know that the key to success is breaking down projects into incremental steps. How can you get a grip on all your various projects and tasks? There is only one way: *you must write them down.*

Start with the Master Task List, which includes literally everything you have to do personally and professionally. Use Appendix C to brainstorm this list. At first, you will tend to group projects and tasks, so use Appendix D as a means of breaking projects down into tasks. Finally, you are ready to move from the Master List (which will, at first glance, appear overwhelming) to your task list for today. You may have more than a hundred "A" priorities on your master list, but you cannot have more than six "A" priorities for today. The "Law of Six" (Reeves, 2002a) does not have a scientific basis, but it certainly yields remarkable consistency. Appendix D provides an example of the Daily Prioritized Task List. Only enter the six "A" priorities that you can realistically accomplish for one day, followed by the Bs and Cs that can be fit into the available pockets of time for the day. Inevitably, interruptions will occur and new priorities will develop, but great time managers do not conflate the vintage of a task with its importance. The oldest tasks may make us feel the most guilty and the newest tasks may have the greatest hold on our enthusiasm, but neither age nor novelty are substitutes for genuine importance.

How do you determine what "important" really means? Covey (1989) and many other authors have suggested that we start with our values. If family is a higher value than money, you will decline a profitable engagement in order to attend a birthday party. If financial security is a higher value than personal pleasure, you will buy a used car and put your savings in a retirement account. Covey's recommendation of a personal mission statement and Smith's recommendation of the creation of a value hierarchy are examples of ways in which each individual can create a framework for decision making and prioritization.

Not every choice is as grand as that between family and work. However, some apparently more mundane choices can have dramatic consequences for time management. For example, I know one senior executive who neither reads nor responds to email on which he is "cc'd," because he does not want to inadvertently validate anyone's attempts to cover various parts of their anatomy by oblique communication with him. "If it's important enough for me to read," he reasons, "then the sender can address me directly." Other effective executives ask this filtering question before adding anything to their DPTLs: Am I the *only* person in this organization who can do this? If they cannot respond in the affirmative to that question, they know that they are robbing someone else of his or her rightful responsibility. Others ask, "What is the consequence if I do not do this?" The executive who stopped responding to copied emails did so without telling anyone in his organization. Three months later, he realized an astonishing thing: no one had even noticed! He had saved hours of time, and the consequence was nil; not a single person who was copying him on emails was begging for his input.

Personal Accountability

Great time managers keep track of their own time as assiduously as hourly employees. Attorneys and accountants bill by the hour, and keep track of their time. Though most consultants bill by the day rather than the hour, the value of each hour—indeed, each minute—is just as important. It's not always possible to write down the starting time of every new activity, but it's not that difficult if you are in the habit of making entries on an Excel spreadsheet or other automated device every hour or two.

Once you record the data, you must analyze it. It's helpful to have a colleague, friend, or spouse (or, in my case, a few thousand readers) with whom you can share these intimate details, warts and all. You cannot expect to be more informed if you do not reallocate time to reading, and that might require reducing time allocated to nonproductive travel. You will not be a published author if you do not reallocate time to research and writing, and that might require reducing time allocated to other things you deeply value, including family. You will not lose that 20 pounds you promised your spouse would be off by December if you do not reallocate time to exercise.

Personal accountability is particularly important for independent consultants because we have no boss, no supervisor, no mentor, and no formal accountability mechanisms. It's just us, and unless you are a person of exceptional discipline and introspection, you will need to develop a method for being accountable for how you invest your time.

Reflection and Planning

Every great time manager values time alone to plan, reflect, revise, and reprioritize. The best time managers make this a daily ritual, typically at the beginning or end of each day. During this time, you not only review your DPTL, but you also periodically take a look at what is really important, including personal and religious philosophies, family ideas, and transcendent values. If you are reading this while you are in a public place, and particularly if you are traveling, take a furtive look around. How many of your fellow travelers appear to be engaged in something that they would say represents the very best use of their time? How many of them appear to be engaged in an activity that reflects their personal values and priorities? On the packed Amtrak Aclea Express from Washington to Boston on which I am writing this chapter, the answer is perhaps two or three. The foursome adjacent to me has been haggling over a business deal for two hours. The man behind them nods in and out of uncomfortable sleep. On the other side are parents who have been delivering unremitting criticism of their child, an exercise that does not seem to be doing any of them much good. The service staff, with one stunning exception, seems distant and disengaged. Would better time management change their lives? Perhaps not, but it might have prompted some of them to reconsider how they spent their time on this trip. If, after every minute, they had to drop a sapphire out the train window, they would savor every facet of that deep blue gem before it vanished forever from their sight. Would that they cherished their time as much as a jewel.

Commitments

Writing it down matters little if you do not do it. Good consultants meet commitments. Great consultants routinely underpromise and overdeliver, exceeding the expectations of every client. The terms *commitment* and *excuse* are mutually exclusive. Meeting commitments means driving all night to make the meeting you promised to attend. Meeting commitments means chartering a jet at a cost three times what you will earn from the client, because your reputation for meeting and exceeding commitments is worth a great deal more than the cost of the charter. Meeting commitments means building a team with the expertise that you do not have and openly acknowledging that you don't know it all.

An essential part of meeting commitments is, of course, knowing what the commitments and expectations are. This involves identification of the real client and completion of detailed pre-engagement conferences, as discussed in Chapter 1. In the real world, clients change their minds, expectations change and increase, and the practices that allowed us to meet today's commitments are the same practices that lead to tomorrow's dissatisfied client.

Commitments involve more than delivering on the contract. Your clients need to be able to assume that you will be on schedule and on budget. Every experienced consultant knows that there is the contract, and then there is *the Contract*. The former is the paper document you signed when good will reigned supreme, you had just beat the competition to get this business, and the client's cooperation ensured your success. The latter agreement—the Contract—is the sum of unexpressed hopes and fears. Whereas the contract gives you dates and deliverables, the Contract assures your clients that you will not embarrass them, that you will help them through the inevitable organizational battles, that you will not blame them when things go wrong, and that you will admit forthrightly and frankly when things go right. Whereas the contract assumes that your commitments are spelled out, definite, and static, the Contract acknowledges that commitments change and grow as your consulting relationship deepens. Whereas the contract is a bilateral agreement between you and your client, the Contract is a reflection of the sum of all your client's experiences with every consultant—wretched and wonderful, diligent and disingenuous, timely and tardy, penny-pinching and profligate. If you want to meet commitments, think not only about the contract, but also about the Contract.

Giving Clients Your Very Best

Your moral, professional, and financial obligation is to give your clients your very best. That means that you arrive well rested, completely informed, and consciously attentive. The client, who is investing a great deal of money in your time, reasonably expects no less. Incredibly, however, consultants routinely dash their clients' reasonable expectations because of misguided attempts at frugality. They promise to arrive well rested and focused, but to save the client $150 in airfare, they take a two-stop, six-hour flight when a direct flight was available. The consultant promises to be attentive, but arrives at the engagement on Monday morning with barely contained fury that she departed on a 6:00 a.m. Sunday-morning flight, and missed a rare family day, just to save the client travel funds. Worse yet, some consultants engage in Saturday stopovers to save client funds, denying themselves and their families the precious rejuvenation time that every human needs. They promised to be well rested, but are bleary-eyed and exhausted because they stayed in a cheap, noisy hotel. The list of penny-wise and pound-foolish travel decisions that consultants make is endless. You owe your clients your very best, so follow these rules.

Use upgrades freely, in the air and on the ground. If you are placed on the upgrade waiting list, call daily and ask the service provider to send your request to "inventory management," who (you hope) will recognize your loyalty and issue you the upgrade. This is not about traveling in style, but about arriving at your destination well rested and well prepared. On airplanes and trains, I either work hard or sleep hard—there is no middle ground. Working hard requires a very small computer and a tray table that does not inflict abdominal injury when the person in front of me reclines the seat. Sleeping hard requires a seat that reclines without inflicting similar injury on the fellow passenger behind me. This doesn't necessarily mean Singapore Airlines international first class, but it may well exclude the middle seat next to a sumo wrestler.

When I land, I don't need a suite, but I do need a quiet and comfortable nonsmoking room. I have hailed taxis or walked several blocks at midnight when a hotel did not have what it promised. I don't need a stretch limo, but I do need a driver who knows how to get to the destination without navigation assistance from me. (Nevertheless, I still take computerized driving instructions for every engagement, every hotel, and every airport, all because I have learned that I cannot safely assume that drivers know how to get to these destinations. Inexplicably, they will ask a hybrid Bostonian-Kansan for directions in Los Angeles.)

To be fair, the real client does not begrudge you reasonable amenities of travel. It is typically someone else in the organization who, often after the fact, will say, "We only allow $11 for breakfast, but you had the $13 buffet," and "Your rental car had a $7-per-day navigation system and we don't pay for that—can't you use a map?" and "You took a limo to the airport and we only approve taxis." That person usually fails to notice that the limo service I use is routinely $5 to $10 cheaper per trip than a taxi. In dealing with clients' financial offices, I have developed a two-word response for these challenges, and it may not be those that are coming into your mind right now. The response is: *No problem*. If there is a $4.75 mini-bar charge on a $700 hotel bill, but I know that the client will not approve alcohol expenditures, then no problem. I make a point of personally circling the offending charge and writing "Do not charge client" on the bill. If the client doesn't want to pay for computerized guidance, no problem; I will. If the comptroller is shocked at the cost of a $50 upgrade on a flight, then no problem; I will pay for it. If the fitness center in the hotel charges $7.50 and the client will not reimburse it, then no problem; I will pay for it.

Perhaps you are thinking that such spendthrift behavior is easy now, but not when one is building a consulting business. Look—I'm not talking about riding into a client's premises on an elephant, accompanied by a retinue of palm-frond-waving servants. I'm not talking about a suite at the Ritz or a magic carpet. I just want some fairly reasonable and inexpensive creature comforts that allow me to be sufficiently rested and give clients my best efforts.

Although the consulting life is a solitary one, some people live such a life by choice, avoiding the challenges of employees and colleagues who can provide strength but also add complications. Others choose to build an organization. I have lived as a consultant in a solo practice and have also built an organization. I share the challenges and rewards of each decision in the next chapter.

7

Organization: Go It Alone or Build an Organization?

The Case for Going It Alone

The Case for Building an Organization

Time: The Consultant's Most Precious Asset

The vast majority of consultants operate as solo practitioners.

They relish their independence, cherish the absence of office

politics, and enjoy the ability to use only pets and plants as a

source of social interaction. They balance the absence of com-

plaints and blissful silence against the concomitant absence of

intellectual challenge, human support, and administrative infra-

structure that an organization might provide.

This chapter examines the advantages and disadvantages of each choice, along with some financial analyses that every consultant must consider before crossing the organizational Rubicon and hiring that first employee.

The Case for Going It Alone

Many consultants are refugees from organizations. They had a successful career, giving their energy, intellect, and personal best to an organization. Then, in the blink of an eye, they went from hero to zero. The best predictor of an impending change in executive leadership, in both public and private organizations, is not the effectiveness of the leader, but a change in the majority of the governing board. Politics, not performance, drives the evaluation of many leaders, and when this equation turns sour, many of those former leaders become consultants who are resolved to remain in an entity in which they are the sole director, executive, and employee. Here, then, are the best reasons to go it alone.

1. Being independent. You will never be told when you can or cannot take a vacation, a day off, or a trip to the dentist. Every fantasy of walking away from your desk can be fulfilled because no one will be summoning you back to your desk. You will never be instructed on the finer points of "business casual" dress because you can eat breakfast and work at your kitchen table in your birthday suit, provided you are very, very careful about your proximity to bacon grease popping from the frying pan.

2. Keeping what you earn. When the solo practitioner bills $1,000, the solo practitioner keeps the whole $1,000 of revenue, except for direct expenses such as office supplies, tax preparation fees, and legal bills. The consultant in a large group typically keeps 30 to 40 percent of gross billings.

3. Choosing your work. Provided that you are exceptionally successful, you can decline work that is tedious and unpleasant. In many group practices, the imperative to meet operating expenses—"covering the nut" in the vernacular of business—requires that many otherwise unappealing but lucrative engagements be accepted. This is why the corporate accountant will do the tax return for a grocery store, why the Harvard-educated lawyer will handle a traffic case, why an ace business consultant will help a small enterprise deal with its accounts receivables, and why a nationally known keynote speaker will sometimes do a workshop for 30 people.

4. Managing your travel. Independent consultants can fly four separate segments from Los Angeles to San Francisco if it is December, and this circuitous route will help earn them a free trip on the airline's enticement of the day. Members of organizations must be more conscious of their time, making every day (indeed, every minute) count for the benefit of the entire firm. Independent consultants can drive their own cars across the country, making every engagement an adventure; members of larger organizations most commonly must endure tray tables and seat backs that are lethal weapons when wielded by clueless adjacent passengers.

5. Building client relationships. Independent consultants can sometimes remain with a single client for weeks on end, even providing services for years. They are one of the family, invited to holiday parties and knowing their colleagues intimately. As a result, the solitary existence of the independent consultant and the absence of collegial relationships is countered by close client relationships. Relationships, however, come to an end, and for the independent consultant who suffers the loss of a major client, the impact can be as traumatic, personally and financially, as if he were an employee who had just been terminated.

6. Avoiding meetings. President John F. Kennedy once greeted a gathering of notable intellectuals who were visiting the White House by saying that he was honored to greet the most exceptional assemblage of intellect ever to have graced the executive mansion—with the possible exception of when Thomas Jefferson was dining alone. Though I have never met a consultant who aspired to that standard of solitary intellectual splendor, I have known many who relish the concept of solitary reflection and who deeply regret the hours wasted in the exercises of collective ignorance, speculation, and gamesmanship that are generally referred to as *meetings*. Although they find relationships with clients and colleagues nice and occasionally stimulating, they generally prefer the pleasure of their own company.

The Case for Building an Organization

The case for building an organization is parallel to that for remaining a solo practitioner. I have lived in both environments. There were certainly times when, as a solo practitioner, I yearned for the support of an organization. There are, nevertheless, days when the burdens of leading an organization make me wistful for the good old days in which I booked every engagement, bought every ticket, reserved every hotel room, and went to Kinko's at 2:00 a.m. to reproduce handouts. The case for an organization follows.

1. Ensuring long-term independence. When the solo practitioner stops working, the enterprise is finished, valueless, an empty revenue stream. When a member of a successful organization stops working, the long-term value remains.

Successful consulting organizations diversify their production base in the same way portfolio managers diversify their stocks, never being excessively exposed to the successes or failures of a single company. In my case, we made a strategic decision to reduce my contribution to company revenues. As Figure 7.1 indicates, we have achieved that objective. In the words of our recent report to our employee-shareholders, "If Dr. Reeves is hit by a bus, we fully expect employees to be sad. We do not, however, expect them to be unemployed."

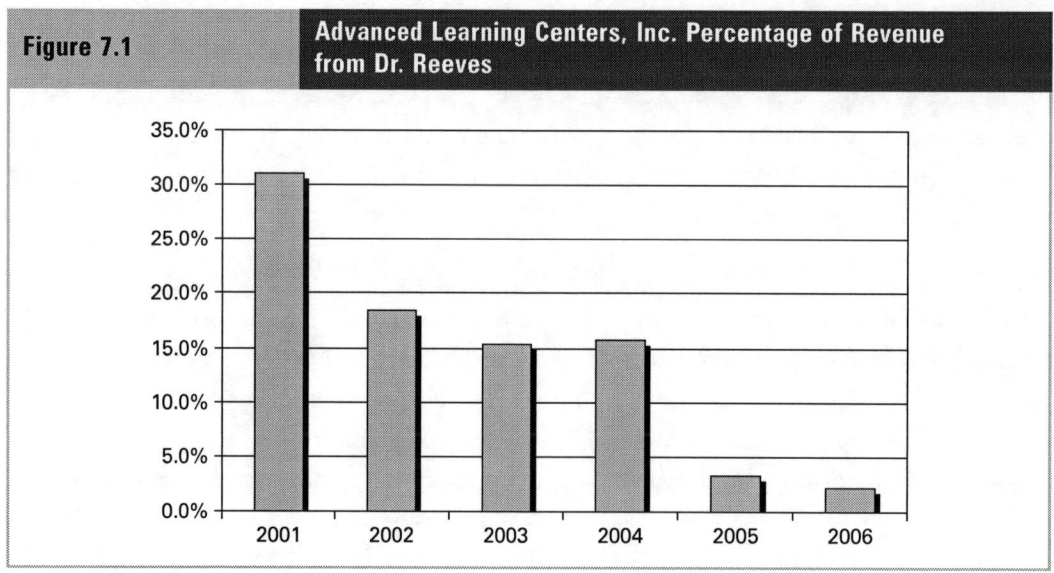

Figure 7.1   **Advanced Learning Centers, Inc. Percentage of Revenue from Dr. Reeves**

Though in the short term every employee in an organization must give up some independence for the greater good of the organization, we provide longer-term benefits that are significant. For example, if a solo practitioner has a baby, a sick child, or an elderly parent, or merely needs a mental health break, revenues come to an immediate halt. In an organization like ours, by contrast, employees can accumulate up to 60 work days (almost three full work months) of paid time off. Only in an organization will paychecks continue when work is temporarily halted.

More importantly, when the solo practitioner retires, the revenue stream evaporates, replaced only by the interest, dividends, and capital gains earned on her retirement accounts. When a member of an organization retires, he not only has pension and profit-sharing plans, but also can have an equity stake in a continuing organization. Our employees all are participants in an employee stock ownership plan (ESOP) that is entirely employer funded.

Finally, social security taxes are very high—more than 15 percent of gross pay—for the self-employed consultant, whereas employees pay 7.2 percent of their earnings into social security. The clear bottom line is that the independent consultant keeps more current income, but potentially sacrifices future equity. Whatever choice you make, there must be a conscious consideration of the future, as both sole practitioners and corporate employees must build retirement plans that do not leave them dependent on social security or the kindness of strangers.

2. Building equity for the future. There is a clear tradeoff between income and equity. If you are independent, you will have the opportunity for higher income. If you are part of an organization, you have the opportunity to build a greater value in organizational equity in the future. If you choose the latter course, it is essential to recognize that the value of your organizational equity is purely a matter of what someone else will pay for it. For the consulting organization, there are four potential sources of equity. First, the large and growing company can go public, selling shares in the public market. Examples of publicly traded consulting companies are Deloitte & Touche LLP, PricewaterhouseCoopers, Ernst & Young International, and KPMG International. Second, equity can be established through selling the value of your holdings to other employees or partners. This is the model on which many legal and accounting firms are based. When the founding partner retires, the remaining partners purchase the departing partner's stake in the organization, usually for a price that has been established by a formal agreement. Third, equity can be established through a formal independent evaluation. Companies that create an ESOP are required by law to use independent evaluations so that the price paid by participating employees is fair. Fourth, the company can sell to another enterprise.

Although each of these options carries some risk, all of them provide greater value to you as the founder of a consulting organization than to you as a solo practitioner. When the solo practitioner retires, the value of the enterprise is comprised solely of the assets of the consulting practice, minus its liabilities. When you quit, the revenues stop and the clients go elsewhere to meet their consulting needs. When you have built an organization, by contrast, the revenue stream continues long after your departure, and therefore the enterprise has a continuing value.

3. Choosing your work. The larger the overhead, the more likely you are to accept engagements that you find distasteful and unpleasant, but that quite literally pay the rent. On this count, solo practitioners appear to have far greater independence than do consultants who build an organization. However, when you build an organization, you are able to delegate engagements to colleagues. You may find a particular engagement to be unappealing, but a colleague may find that it fits her skills perfectly.

Also, clients sometimes magnify their perceptions of a consultant's abilities: "She did such a great job in human resources—let's ask her to help us on sales and marketing!" "He was great as a keynote speaker—let's have him do a three-day workshop!" Only the most extraordinary self-discipline will prevent the solo consultant from saying, "Sure, I can do that." When you have built an organization, you can say, "We very much want to meet your needs, but this request is outside my personal area of expertise. Fortunately, I have a colleague who specializes in this area, so let us work as a team to meet your needs."

4. Managing your travel. Organizations—either the client or the consulting enterprise—can place restrictions on travel that elevate frugality over common sense. The stereotype is that the independent consultant can use upgrades profligately, while the organizational slave sits in steerage and doesn't even collect the frequent flier miles for the trip. If you choose to build an organization, my counsel would be that you think every day of how your employees would answer the question, "Am I better off with this organization or alone?" As the creator of a consulting organization, your unending obligation is to ensure that your very best employees answer that question with an enthusiastic commitment to remain in your organization. In my company, we lavish rewards on "Century Club" members—those consultants who have more than 100 days each year on the road. They receive free airline club memberships, free first-class upgrades, expense allowances for their home offices, and professional development scholarships. They keep their own frequent flier miles and regularly treat their families to spectacular vacations for little or no cost. In other words, our most productive consultants are made to feel that they have every advantage they would have if they were operating independently, and perhaps even more.

5. Building relationships. This is a key distinction between the solo practitioner and the consulting organization. For the solo consultant, the primary relationship is between the client and the person, and that relationship is, by definition, personal. For the consulting organization, the relationship with the client is organizational. If one consultant cannot make an engagement due to illness or travel delays, another consultant with equal qualifications will meet the commitment.

For the solo practitioner, the client may regard the work as the "Smith plan" because consultant Smith was the chief architect of the project. For the successful consulting organization, names of individuals are deliberately and consistently subordinated to that of the organization. Even in great consulting firms that bear the name of their founder, such as McKinsey & Company, the client relationships are not with the late Mr. McKinsey, but with the firm. One of the most difficult lessons in organizational growth is that the founder must let go of the solo practitioner mentality whereby a single consultant solves every problem, meets every need, and swoops in to save the day whenever the client expresses a need. The organization will never grow if the founder is the dominant consultant for a client engagement. Clients will be perpetually dissatisfied if they feel that they are being passed off from one consultant to another.

The only way successful relationships are built between organizations is when the consulting enterprise takes a team approach to relationship building from the very start. Gently, firmly, and consistently, the consultant helps clients to understand that the relationship is not with a person, but with an organization. In my case, I do not work with clients unless they have partnership relationships with our company, using other consultants far more frequently than they use me during the year. I have seen other very successful consultants cheerfully decline engagements, telling the astonished client, "I only work when the client is serious about making major improvements, and that will require a major commitment, not a one-day engagement."

6. Meetings. There is no question that meetings are a part of organizational growth. Even in well-run and highly disciplined organizations, meetings can wander away from their intended purposes, devolve into political posturing, and generally constitute a colossal waste of individual and organizational time. These risks are, I would argue, not a case against meetings, but a case against poorly planned and badly executed meetings. If you are the creator of a consulting company, you have only yourself to blame if you allow meetings to proliferate, deviate, and dissemble. As the leader of your organization, you have the ability to say, "I don't think we're ready to have a productive meeting, so let's gather again next week when we have a better command of the facts and are ready to invest our time wisely." This sounds perilously close to the expectation that consultants will follow the advice they would give to clients — a rare event indeed.

Time: The Consultant's Most Precious Asset

Perhaps the most important determining factor in your decision to remain independent or to build an organization is how you will spend your time. Having lived as a solo practitioner — answering the phone, doing the books, sending the invoices, making the collection calls, booking the travel, and attending to every single detail of the business and consulting life — I made a conscious decision that the risks of building an organization were outweighed by the rewards of having other people do these things for me so that I could devote my energies to what I do best: working with clients. I also recognize that there are days when I volunteer in school, nights when I watch a movie with my family, and weekends when I walk by the ocean, all of which would have been consumed by the hours required to do administrative tasks if I were a solo practitioner. Building an organization is not the only valid choice, but it is the choice that was right for me.

In contrast, I have many friends who have built successful consulting enterprises and have remained independent. Some have aligned themselves with service bureaus that handle their billings, booking, and travel. Others hire personal assistants but otherwise keep their organizational overhead to a minimum. At the end of the day, this decision will not be based solely on economic considerations, but on personal ones. The decision to remain on your own or to build an organization will influence how you invest your income, energy, and time.

Quality: Defining Your Competitive Advantage

Standards for Success

Essential Questions

RCI: Return on Consulting Investment

The Crowding-Out Phenomenon

The quality of professional consulting services is too frequently measured by popularity rather than effectiveness. This is particularly true when consulting work involves formal presentations, training, and seminars. Despite the claims of training vendors that they provide a return on investment, an astonishingly high percentage of these programs are evaluated on the degree to which a good time was had by all. Factors such as refreshments, location, creature comforts, and presentation humor factor more heavily in the equation than business results.

Goleman and his colleagues (Goleman, Boyatzis & McKee, 2002) were dismayed to find that many popular corporate programs yielded a minimal to negative return on investment, whereas less popular and barely respectable programs on business basics such as time management showed an exceptionally high return.

The fundamental argument of this chapter is that consulting relationships that last are based on clear expectations and measurable results. When you embrace this level of accountability, you will deliver great service to your clients, set extraordinary standards for yourself and your colleagues, and create high RCI (return on consulting investment). A high RCI is what allows you to sleep at night, knowing that whatever you charge, you brought more value to your client than the cost of your fees. A high RCI allows you to appropriately value your time, hire an assistant, invest in technology, and insist on the collaboration that is essential to make an effective client-consultant partnership work.

Standards for Success

At the heart of any consideration of quality is the issue of standards. What are your expectations for a perfect client engagement? Take a moment to reflect on your personal view of perfection, and then compare every engagement to that personal view. Figure 8.1 will help you identify your personal standards.

You will get the most out of this exercise if you work from the inside out—that is, start with the "proficient" column and describe the components of an engagement that is perfectly adequate, but otherwise unremarkable. Then fill in the next column, describing an engagement that is "progressing"—close to what you want, but still missing the mark. Then describe an engagement that is wretched and, in almost every sense, a colossal failure. Finally, complete the "exemplary" column to describe in vivid and explicit terms the components of an engagement that is an extraordinary success.

This process may seem cumbersome, but it is essential. You cannot achieve exceptional quality if you do not first create a clear vision of what a superior level of quality looks like. Moreover, the progression from poor to superior performance does not take place in a single leap. Human performance almost always takes place along a continuum. We do not ask the five-minute miler to run a four-minute mile without undertaking a number of adjustments that yield four-plus-minute times. We do not ask the novice pilot to proceed from a single-engine aircraft to flying a Boeing 747; we acknowledge that there are many things to learn about the complexities of multiengine

Figure 8.1	The Perfect Engagement	
Characteristic	**Consultant Actions**	**Client Actions**
1. Pre-engagement planning		
2. Presentation to client		
3. Interaction with client		
4. Application of client data		
5. Client follow-up and decisionmaking processes		
6. Other characteristics of a perfect engagement		

aircraft, jet propulsion, air traffic control, and hundreds of other incremental steps between these two aviation challenges. The difference between good consulting work and superior work is a multifaceted challenge. Take a moment to describe performance in each area that is important to you.

Now that you have described consulting performance in your own terms, consider how other people have responded to the same challenge. Figure 8.2 illustrates how some people have described superior performance.

Figure 8.2 — Consultant Self-Evaluation

Professional Development Presentation Scoring Guide

Characteristic of Effective Presentation	Exemplary	Proficient	Progressing	Not Meeting Standard	Observations and Suggestions for Improvement
1. Preparation	Firm checklist completed. Handouts to client two weeks before presentation; backup slides ready; room and sound system checked one hour before presentation.	Checklist completed. Handouts to client one week before presentation; no backup slides, but you will readily bet that the projector will work; sound system and room checked 15 minutes before presentation.	Checklist incomplete; handouts made it—barely.	Showed up late; handouts lost in mail; projector didn't work; slides out of order; thrown tomatoes hit their mark.	
2. Visual Presentation	Slides all have firm logo; all slides are numbered; every slide has text that is clearly visible by 1,000 people in a lighted room. When projector is in use, PowerPoint animation features are used to emphasize individual bullet points, and remote control (with spare battery handy) works flawlessly. The slides are perfectly organized and flow logically. The presentation includes the firm's standard "administrative notes" as well as a clear indication of overview, organization, context, and expectations. Audience members are overheard saying of the quality of your visuals, "The Louvre was good, but this is *great*."	Slides all have logo; all are numbered, and text is clearly visible. The sequence is well organized and has the standard administrative and organizational elements.	Slides lack logo and/or numbering. Organizational and administrative slides are missing.	What slides?	
3. Oral Presentation	The people said, "Let us march." The wireless microphone (with a new battery inside and a spare in your pocket) works flawlessly. Your voice is clear, confident, distinct, and comprehensible by people whose primary language is not English. Your voice is animated, with contrasts in pitch, rate, volume, and intensity. The audience is overheard saying, "I didn't think it was possible to combine Jerry Seinfeld and John Housman in the same character."	The people said, "How well he speaks." You wowed 'em, but that's what they paid for. The microphone was fine and the variation in pitch, rate, volume, and intensity was professional. It lacked nothing except the "je ne sais quoi."	The people said, "One more staff development meeting—ho hum." You had to replace the battery or deal with distracting noises in the system. Your pace was solid, but overly consistent. You were rushed, or seemed wooden.	The people said, "Another waste of time in the guise of an expert." The frequency on the wireless microphone was mixed so that they saw you but heard Bill Daggett in the adjoining room. People said, "I always wondered what the dummy looked like without the ventriloquist."	

Professional Development Presentation Scoring Guide

Characteristic of Effective Presentation	Exemplary	Proficient	Progressing	Not Meeting Standard	Observations and Suggestions for Improvement
4. Participant Engagement	No more than 20 minutes passed without direct audience engagement. The only complaint was that "there wasn't enough time and we wish we had more, more, more." The audience engagement varied from clear questions that elicited meaningful and immediate responses, to thought-provoking case studies that allowed individual and small group work to yield significant insights. Participants left with a clear action plan that was directly and immediately relevant to their personal and professional circumstances.	Some engagement, but the weight was on pre-sentation. Questions were appropriate and elicited good responses.	Questions were controlled and contrived.	What questions—didn't they come to listen to me preach?	
5. Content	Cutting-edge educational policy, including new and original research that the firm has conducted, recent research from leaders in the field, and an obvious grasp of the subject matter. Clear acknowledgement of the research and theoretical shoulders on which you stand, combined with genuinely original insights into your subject. Yes, it's relevant to the client, but it's also relevant to the professional world of educators. You combine respect for the audience (avoiding blinding flashes of the obvious) with a healthy skepticism about the level of research and background that participants have in the subject. Thirty-year veteran educators, researchers, and professors leave the program saying, "I didn't know that!" and are reinvigorated about the process of learning new things.	Educational policy and research that is firmly grounded in contemporary research, appropriately credited to others and to the firm, and relevant to the client's needs. The presentation contains 3–4 explicit references to data and examples from the client.	The content met the billing of the advertisement— but if someone were to seriously ask if this presentation were any different from a thousand others, we'd offer a shrug and show them our return plane ticket.	All they want to see is your return plane ticket.	
6. Service	You got out of the limelight and into a classroom, spending time with real teachers and students. This wasn't part of the agenda, but you did it so as to continue your own education, test your generalizations, and give encouragement to students and teachers who needed it. You made personal contacts with whom you can continue an important dialog in the future.	You provided on-the-spot reviews and evaluations of the client's work, offered constructive suggestions for improvement, and gave them the "extra mile" of service and assistance that they have a right to expect from a consultant.	You thought that speaking for an extra 15 minutes was a great service.	You thought that speaking 15 minutes less was a great service.	
7. Evaluation	Real-time feedback from participants was used to modify and improve your presentation. You added agenda items on the computerized overhead based on participant feedback, and had handouts produced during a break that directly and specifically reflected participant contribution and feedback. In other words, you modeled the process of using assessment and feedback from students to influence instruction.	Some adjustments—prin-cipally by omitting slides or adding spontaneous and extended responses based on participant questions.	You delivered it as it was canned—no more, no less.	Ignored obvious signals from participants; unable/unwilling to change and improve.	

Finally, consider the advice of Peter Block, author of the classic work, *The Flawless Consulting Fieldbook* (2001), who wrote the following words after decades of successful consulting. Block reminds us that successful consulting is not only about logistical details or technical expertise. Rather, we must consider that every change recommendation has an emotional price that clients must pay, even when they do not expect it. If the client asks the consultant to address a problem, the least popular, but most necessary, words the consultant may speak will address the client's role in the creation and sustenance of that problem. In Block's words:

> *The key for consultants is to be willing and able to face the fundamental and most troubling questions facing our clients. These are most often emotional issues; they involve problems of control, integrity, vulnerability, and relationship, and they represent an area no one enters lightly.*
>
> *Our reluctance to confront our clients with their own personal contribution to the problems they face meets with their wish to look far outside themselves for answers. This combination results in change efforts that ultimately disappoint (p. 73).*

Essential Questions

In my consulting firm, we ask three questions after every engagement. First, "On a scale of 1 to 10, with 10 being the best you have ever experienced, did our work achieve your organizational objective?" In our case, that means improving student achievement. In the case of other consulting organizations, the organizational objective might include profitability, employee satisfaction, improvements in efficiency, and so on. The key is that we must ask about the degree to which our services influenced organizational results.

I have frequently been challenged on this question. Colleagues will say, "Wait a minute—we did all we could do, but it's up to the client to actually implement our advice. How can we be held accountable for their actions?" My rejoinder is clear: If we are not responsible for client results, then why were we there? Were we just an act booked for the purpose of entertainment, or did we really commit to help them achieve their objectives? Your relationship with your client and your ability to deliver valuable services in an ethical manner all depend on your willingness to associate your work with client results. If you are a sales consultant, it is reasonable to hold yourself accountable for improved sales. If you are a technology consultant, you must have concrete ways to show how you improved efficiency, reduced costs, improved service, or otherwise achieved measurable business results.

The second essential question is, "On a scale of 1 to 10, with 10 being the best you have ever experienced, did we meet your expectations?" The response to this question helps us understand the real needs of the client, and they are not often what we originally understood when the engagement was planned. For example, it is entirely possible to achieve a high score on the first question—meeting client objectives—but a lower score on the second question regarding the client's expectations. How can that be?

Consider this example: The client wanted to significantly improve the accountability and evaluation system. We helped to do that, providing improved informal and formal assessment programs and comprehensive training to implement the new programs. We even linked the new accountability systems to improved results throughout the client's organization. However, the client's real expectations went far beyond achieving improved results. The client also wanted to be loved and appreciated by his subordinates, peers, and board members. That did not happen. In fact, some of the improvements in accountability and results created organizational friction, jealousies, and backbiting. Were we successful? Certainly. Did we meet the client's unspoken expectations? Not a chance. In fact, had we done a better job of learning about this hidden client need, we could have managed expectations much better, alerting the client to the very high probability that even a successful accountability and evaluation system would be met with resistance. We could have said at the beginning of the engagement, "I must warn you—this won't be popular and even if you are successful, there will be a price to pay in personal relationships." Such a discussion would not have made it any easier for this client to suffer the slings and arrows of organizational dysfunction, but at least we would have avoided the surprise our client suffered. This was our fault: we failed to ask enough questions, to listen better, and to understand the difference between the stated objective and the hidden objectives. Great consultants know both sets of objectives, and asking our quality control questions will help us do a better job in the future.

The third question is, "On a scale of 1 to 10, with 10 being the best you have ever experienced, how was the support you received from our administrative staff?" The client's perception of the quality of an engagement is a function not only of the ability of the consultant, but also of the way in which the details of the engagement are handled. At least once a week, I hear a client remark about how extraordinary our staff is, double- and triple-checking details, providing superior logistical support, and generally giving clients confidence that their interests are being looked after in an exceptional manner. This creates the presumption of success before I set foot in the door. Clients know that they are dealing with a professional organization because our administrative staff gives them that impression.

If you are starting in this profession, you may question this third quality question. "Administrative staff? What administrative staff?" In fact, many successful consultants operate without any support staff. They book their own reservations, send their own invoices, make their own collection calls, and keep their own books. Sometimes they do this because they are attempting to control costs; others simply wish to avoid the potential problems of dealing with employees and a growing organization. Having worked alone, with a very small support team, and in a large organization, I can only offer this advice. If you are really good at what you do, and if you really enjoy what you do as a consultant, then it does not make any sense for you to voluntarily spend time doing anything else. One of your first investments should be in an assistant, even if it is only for ten hours each week. A great assistant is your voice to the outside world, the one who will help you be successful, who will reduce your stress, who will talk to clients about money when you prefer not to, who will make you look like a million dollars to your clients, who will save your bacon in a thousand different ways. A great assistant who works for a few hours a week, if paid an excellent hourly rate (what do you pay your plumber or electrician?), will be an investment in your professional future.

Whether you remain a sole practitioner or build an organization, the answers to these three questions provide a gold mine of information. They will give you insight into your clients, their objectives, their needs, their peculiarities, and, most importantly, your opportunities to serve clients better. Our standard, which is the standard of any world-class organization, is to achieve a "10"—a "best we have ever experienced"—rating for every engagement on every question. Do we achieve it? No. In fact, I maintain a running average of these numbers, and the responses for the past year are as follows:

Meeting client objectives:	9.2%
Meeting client expectations:	9.2%
Administrative support:	9.5%

Whenever a rating is lower than a 7, I personally call the client and find out what went wrong. We jump through every imaginable hoop to make clients satisfied and restore their confidence. On a scale of 1 to 10, 6 is an abject failure for a quality-driven organization. We also track these numbers for each individual consultant and for each individual team and hold ourselves mutually accountable for the results.

RCI: Return on Consulting Investment

As important as the quality numbers are, there is an even more important number that every consultant must know. What is your RCI? That is, what is your return on consulting investment? This number allows you to make an essential claim to every client: The most expensive organizational gamble is a cheap consultant. In Chapter 5, I suggested that you follow the "better free than cheap" rule. Now is the time when we put our money where our mouths are. We say that our consulting services are worth the price, so let us demonstrate it. There are two ways to calculate RCI, either as a one-year return or as a more complex multiyear return. The simple formula for RCI is as follows:

$$RCI = \text{net positive cash flow} \div \text{consulting cost}$$

Let's apply this formula to a realistic example. Assume for a moment that you are a quality control consultant. You can't work miracles, but you can quite consistently improve the quality of customer relation databases by 10 percent. Even a small company such as ours has about 50,000 names in its database. We send them each a catalog twice a year; the combined mailing and production cost of each catalog is about $1, for a total cost of $100,000. If your processes, training, and procedures improve the quality of our database by 10 percent, then you are saving us $10,000 per year. If you charge us $20,000 for your expertise, we can easily apply the RCI formula:

$$RCI = \$10,000 \div \$20,000$$
$$RCI = 50\% \text{ annually}$$

It would take us two years of $10,000 savings to get our consulting costs back; after that, we are earning a net 50 percent return on our consulting investment. Most consultant investments are more complicated, requiring a more subtle analysis of the return on investment. Microsoft Excel provides an excellent and fast way to calculate what financial analysts call "internal rate of return," or "IRR" in the vernacular of the trade.

Starting with the same example, in which your quality control efforts saved the client $10,000 per year for five years, for a cost of only $20,000, the real return is more than 50 percent. The IRR function of your spreadsheet analysis allows you to quantify the RCI and take into account the time in which the investment will be repaid. To perform this calculation, you must know the following information:

1. **The investment in consultant services.** This is entered as a negative number on the spreadsheet.

2. **The positive cash flow resulting from your services.** You generate positive cash flow from cost savings, improved revenues, increased efficiency, or, as in the example above, improved quality.

3. **The time horizon to be considered by the client.** Although consultants frequently prefer to analyze the results of their work in the long term, and quote authorities on systemic change who argue that effective long-term change

requires five to seven years, we would be wise to recall the famous words of the economist John Maynard Keynes, who said, "In the long run we are all dead."

Once you have these three pieces of information, you can make the spreadsheet entries such as those shown in Figure 8.3.

Figure 8.3		RCI—Multiyear Return on Consulting Investment		
Cell 1	Column A	Column B	Column C	Column D
Cell 2	Year	Investment	Positive Cash Flow	Net Cash Flow
Cell 3	1	−20,000	10,000	−10,000
Cell 4	2		10,000	10,000
Cell 5	3		10,000	10,000
		Internal Rate of Return:	62%	

Figure 8.3 shows an example of the spreadsheet entries. In Column B, we list the investment in consulting as a negative number; shown in the example as −$20,000. If there were annual consulting expenses, we would list those for each year as well. In Column C, we list the net positive cash flow to the client—savings, income, or other cash flow that resulted from your work. In the example, the services led to a cost savings of $10,000 each year for five years. Column D is the sum of the first two—the net cash flow. If you spent more than you saved, the fourth column is a negative number. If you saved more than you spent, the fourth column is a positive number. Finally, the return on investment is calculated automatically using this entry:

=IRR([column name of the net cash flow],estimated return)

In this example, the net cash flow is in column D, and the three years the client would consider for return on investment purposes are represented in cells D3, D4, and D5. My first estimated return, based on the simple formula with which we started, was 50 percent. Therefore, my entry in the computer was: = IRR([D4:D6],.5). The result? 62 percent, an even better return than the client expected.

Try your own exercises with the simple and multiyear formulas. In a matter of seconds, you can see how increased savings for the client will justify higher investments in consulting. You will also clearly see that increased consulting costs without improved client cash flow will give the client an excellent reason for declining to use your services. A good RCI is necessary in every context, whether your clients are profit-making businesses, governmental entities, or nonprofit organizations. Every client has finite resources that must be allocated in a way that best serves the interest of its owners or other stakeholders. Great consultants prove, in an objective and clear manner, that they create a return on investment. This is true not only in the examples we have already cited, where cost savings were clear, but for soft skills as well. If you can help managers develop interpersonal skills, evaluation mechanisms, or interviewing techniques that will reduce turnover from 20 percent to 15 percent, you can easily calculate the value of those "soft" skills. Turnover costs money—easily one-third of the cost of an employee's annual wages and an untold cost in employee morale. Even a small organization with $2 million in payroll will find that a 20 percent turnover costs one-third of 20 percent of $2 million, or $132,000. If your consulting services reduce turnover to 15 percent, you reduced turnover costs to one-third of 15 percent of $2 million, or $99,000—a net savings of $33,000 each year. Does that make your $20,000 management training program sound like a bargain?

The Crowding-Out Phenomenon

When you gain a consulting engagement, you do more than provide services to your client. You also prevent someone else—your competitor—from using those same resources of time, money, and executive attention. Prevention of the misuse of resources may be as important as the wise use of resources that are directed toward paying for your services. In the course of your needs analysis, you will have learned about the other consultants your prospective client has used. If you take a careful inventory of those consulting services, you will discover that many clients have engaged a series of consultants, many of whom give inconsistent and contradictory messages. Their efforts form the opposite of synergy, in which their collective work not only fails to generate an impact that is greater than the sum of their work, but also drains resources and promotes cynicism throughout the client organization. These people may not be malicious, but they are not serving the client's interest.

We have declined engagements when it was clear that our work would be fragmentary and unproductive because the client was too deeply committed to other consultants with contradictory messages. Some of our most successful engagements have been where we have started in an environment of multiple consultants: as the documented effectiveness of our efforts increased, the client winnowed the field and concentrated more resources, time, and leadership focus on fewer efforts. By crowding out the competition, we not only achieved business success, but also served the clients better and helped them allocate their limited resources wisely.

As you infuse quality throughout your consulting efforts, you will be rewarded with an increasing demand for your services. This success comes with a price in terms of the complexity of your personal and professional lives. In the next chapter, we consider the reality of the consulting life, and I will share lessons I have learned about the organizational and family life of a practicing consultant.

CHAPTER 9

Reality: Lessons from the Field

Growth

Replication

Employee Ownership

Retaining Great People

Respect for Individual Needs

Although I have built a successful consulting practice, I have also made many mistakes along the way. This chapter includes the lessons not only of my successes, but of my mistakes as well. Whether you intend to establish a solo practice or build an organization, you must confront many critical decisions. You, your clients, your employees, and your family will be better served if you anticipate those critical decisions now.

Growth

You must grow. Although the domestic inflation rate is at historically low levels now, there are very important expenses in your life—medical care, college tuition, and energy, to name a few—for which the annual cost increases significantly outpace inflation. Moreover, because investment returns in the twenty-first century are significantly lower than they were in the 1990s, you must put aside more money today than would have been required 20 years ago to provide for your own retirement and your family's financial security. Many consultants kid themselves into believing that "I can slow down any time I want" or "Some day I'll have it made, I'll work fewer hours, and take only selected clients." Even if that enchanting future awaits you, the reality will not change: either you must increase your revenues every year, or you must reduce your expenses. You cannot choose to reduce your working hours or client relationships without reducing tuition payments (or savings for future tuition payments), reducing medical costs (or savings for future medical costs), or cutting back on your consumption of oil, gas, and electricity. This is not to say that you must achieve double-digit growth rates, or that you must drive revenue growth beyond the capacity of yourself and your organization, but you must have a plan to grow on a systematic and regular basis. Otherwise, your consulting enterprise and your personal finances will fail.

There are four principal ways to increase consulting revenues. First and most obviously, just work harder. If you start by making $500 for a day and have an open calendar, income will be maximized if you fill the calendar. Ten days a month generates more income than five; by the same logic, thirty days are twice as lucrative as fifteen. However, there is an obvious limit here, and wise consultants learn that limit well before they hit the mental, physical, and emotional wall called *exhaustion*. This limit is particularly close when each day of work also means a trip to a different city, another time zone, another hotel room, and another day away from home. Working harder, though a rational response to client needs and your desire to grow your enterprise, is not a sustainable model for growth.

Second, consultants can increase their revenues by increasing their fees. We do this every year, starting on our new fiscal year, July 1. The increases are incremental, typically 3 to 7 percent per year. Clients expect it, just as they see other prices of everything from electricity to water to paper increase. We have found that it is much easier to deal with small annual increases than to keep prices stable for several years and then, in the fourth or fifth year, try to catch up with what appears to the client to be a massive and sudden increase.

Consulting fees are the price of services, established not solely by the consultant, but by the market in which a willing buyer and seller agree on a price. Very rarely, we have consultants who can receive very substantial annual increases—from 20 to 50 percent in a single year—typically because the demand for their services has soared. Demand in the consulting business might be fueled by the exceptional value-added reputation of a particular consultant, her notoriety due to publishing or speaking, or simply the rapid spread of her reputation by word of mouth. In contrast, we have had consultants for whom an annual increase was not justified. Both the large increase and the zero increase are rare, however, and the wisest course of action is a planned set of annual fee increases that allow consultants to keep pace with inflation; such increases also recognize that with each year of experience, consultants should be bringing additional insight and value to every client engagement. Your ability to increase your fees, however, is entirely dependent on the supply-demand balance in your part of the consulting industry. With a generation of baby boomers becoming eligible for retirement, but far too young to quit working, the number of people offering consulting services is set to explode. If that happens in your industry, supply could easily outpace demand, keeping a lid on your ability to increase fees without losing revenues. Therefore, you will need to consider the final two revenue growth strategies.

The third model for revenue growth involves altering the product/service mix. Consider Jennifer Epstein, a consultant who takes 100 paid engagement days per year at $1,000 per day. She isn't loafing the other 265 days every year; instead, she's learning, researching, listening, and exploring her industry for new clients. She also is raising a family, and enjoys spending time at home and volunteering in community activities. Therefore, 100 days is about the maximum she is willing to put into her consulting career. For the last several years, Jennifer's revenues have stagnated, though $1,000 per day for 100 days seemed like a good living, with friends envying her apparent six-figure income. Still, with a mortgage, payments on a modest car, braces for three kids, and the need to save for college and retirement, it is readily apparent that she is falling behind.

If Jennifer pursues the first growth model—more days on the road—she fears that she will fall into the same trap that has destroyed the health and families of some of her friends. All the money in the world is worth little if stress ruins your health and preoccupation destroys your marriage. Over the past year, however, Jennifer has noticed that she has been spontaneously creating a number of tools for clients. These simple tools include paper forms that clients use to follow up on her advice and training; simple Microsoft Excel, Access, and PowerPoint applications that clients use to sustain Jennifer's efforts long after she has left the office; and even some crudely done audio- and videotapes that help clients remember what she did. Because she is committed to great client service, Jennifer created these tools knowing that she was adding value, but without ever giving much thought to the creation of those tools in a systematic way.

None of these tools is very fancy, but together they form the Jennifer Epstein Tool Kit. She assembled a sample version of it, even creating a box decorated like a tool kit to contain the paper forms, DVD, audio cassette, and CD-ROM with the spreadsheet, database, and presentation software applications that she had created. When Jennifer showed her samples to clients—the very people to whom she had previously provided her tools for free—they were thrilled, asking only, "What does it cost?" Jennifer hesitated, because the cost of the materials was minimal (less than $10 per kit), and the cost of the video and audio production had been less than $5,000 (only about $5 for each of the 1,000 kits she had created). Jennifer had seen similar tool kits from major business schools and consulting firms sell for hundreds of dollars, but they had much fancier packaging and better-known brand names than the "Jennifer Epstein Tool Kit." Trying to provide reasonable value for her clients but nevertheless reward herself for her creativity and work, Jennifer tentatively said, "They are $49 each, with a 25 percent discount for orders of ten or more." Her client astonished Jennifer by responding, "We've been ordered to cut back on consulting costs, so I don't know if I can continue to increase the days we have you work with us. But with this tool kit, we can get a lot more done and save money next year. I'll take one for each of the 42 people in my department." Even with the 25 percent discount, this single sale brought in more than $1,500. If only one-tenth of her consulting days yielded similar results, Jennifer would add more than $15,000 to her annual revenues without working a single extra day.

In fact, Jennifer was already envisioning ways to create other tools that would deliver great value to clients and provide a continuing revenue stream for herself, all without adding a single travel day to her schedule. Note that Jennifer did not write a best-selling business book or develop the next great computer program. She just delivered simple tools that clients could use. She focused on the strengths she already had and the needs that she knew her clients had. This simple and direct approach to innovation is not the "disruptive innovation" (Christensen, 2003) that leads to the next blockbuster in pharmaceuticals or technology. Jennifer's incremental, low-tech strategy did, however, provide precisely what her clients needed, and also allowed Jennifer to continue revenue growth without either raising prices or increasing her consulting days.

The fourth, and most complex, path to revenue growth is *replication*. As Jennifer's example illustrates, replication of paper, computer disks, and DVDs is simple: just print more and ship them out. Replication of human effort is a decidedly more challenging issue. It is not just a matter of hiring more people. The key to replication is having the consultant define precisely what those other people do, and training them to follow that model with fidelity. This rarely happens. Sometimes the person who created the idea is one who operates with an intuitive grasp of the issues, making keen insights, getting to the heart of client issues, developing perfect strategies, and communicating all of this in a winsome and engaging way—but this same person cannot explain how he did what he did. I've interviewed some world-class consultants who are beloved by clients and who regularly astound people with their insights. When I try to get them to articulate what they did and how they did it, the answers include "I listen well," or "I did my homework," or "I just helped the clients articulate what they already knew." All three of these explanations may be perfectly valid, but they are the reason that so few world-class consulting models can be replicated.

Every Sunday, the *New York Times Magazine* has a fascinating story about the diagnosis of a patient's mysterious symptoms. Invariably, the path from patient complaint to final diagnosis is circuitous, requiring the knowledge, skill, wisdom, insight, and sometimes just plain luck of one or more diagnosticians. Although machines can conduct many laboratory tests, and computer programs can suggest inferences that a physician might draw, the definitive diagnosis remains a human interaction between doctor and patient. The safe return of a damaged spacecraft from lunar orbit, documented in the film *Apollo 13,* reminds us that technological miracles are unsustainable without human judgment. Given the complexity of identifying, documenting, and repeating complex human judgments, how does replication happen in a consulting firm? That is the subject of the next section.

Replication

Replication is an extraordinarily complex challenge. Even in manufacturing, a single detail among hundreds of processes can spell the difference between acceptable quality and life-threatening mistake. The winter flu season of 2004–2005 was abnormal, not because of the severity of the flu (a malady that strikes thousands of people annually), but because of the failure of manufacturing quality control processes for flu vaccine, which placed in jeopardy the lives of infants, seniors, and hundreds of thousands of others who were most vulnerable to the flu virus. Quality defects in automobiles, consumer appliances, and buildings are daily reminders of how frequently even the most stringent quality control procedures fail. When it comes to replication of human consulting processes, the challenge is not merely to duplicate the assembly line, but to replicate the engineer; not merely to rebuild the spacecraft, but to replicate the astronaut; not merely to produce the vaccine, but to replicate the physicians and researchers who developed it.

There are three elements of replication: systems, knowledge base development, and integration. In *The E-Myth Revisited* (2001), Michael Gerber explained that great organizations have written systems for everything they do. It is as important to have a written system for reconciling your business checkbook every month as it is to have a written system for transforming a casual acquaintance at a business meeting into a multiyear client. Each time you respond, "That's easy—anybody can do it!" or "I can't really explain what I did—it just happened!," you are denying yourself the opportunity to create a system and, as a result, preventing any possibility of replication in your organization. Take note the next time you are in a particularly well-maintained restroom in an airport, convenience store, or other public facility. You will very likely find a document somewhere, perhaps posted visibly, that bears the initials of a person who personally inspected that restroom and the time the inspection was done. If you have ever worked in a successful restaurant, whether it was a national fast-food franchise or an haute cuisine establishment, you know that systems abound for everything from the time French fries are cooked to the way vegetables are sautéed. You cannot replicate without systems, and you cannot grow without replication. The pre-engagement checklist (Appendix A) is an example of a system, guaranteeing that you will get the same information in the same way for every client. Take a moment to list the processes that are most important to your consulting organization and enter them in Figure 9.1.

For each of these, create a clear and detailed system. Even if you are the only person using the system now, the establishment and documentation of effective systems will prepare your organization for future replication and growth. Systems also provide a level of quality and consistency that your clients will appreciate. Furthermore, systems help you avoid disasters. Recently I was scheduled to speak before a very large audience at a major conference. The client called me and said, "When we booked you, your office meticulously confirmed every detail and followed up regularly, so we knew we could count on you. You even had a pre-engagement conference so that we knew you were tailoring your remarks to the needs of our group. But just today another speaker now claims that we had booked him and he was counting on the date. But he never called, never sent us any written acknowledgment, and never contacted us until a few weeks before the conference. He's very upset with us, but we just can't use him." Our systems and our consistent implementation of these systems helped us avoid what could have been a very embarrassing situation.

Figure 9.1	System Development

Instructions: List your professional and business processes here. Ultimately, you will create a system for every process. Enter the date as you complete each system. Remember, you cannot replicate your consulting practices without systems, and you cannot grow without replication.

1.0   Client Development Processes: **System Complete Date**

1.1

1.2

1.3

1.4

2.0   Client Service Processes:

2.1

2.2

2.3

2.4

3.0   Financial Processes:

3.1

3.2

3.3

3.4

4.0   Technology Processes:

4.1

4.2

4.3

4.4

Other processes:

Examples of other potential systems appear in Appendices B and E. System creation can be a daunting task. It is easy to succumb to the complaint (excuse), "If I really write a system for everything I should, it would take two years!" That may well be true; I am still writing new systems many years after creating the first one for my organization. The relevant question, however, is this: What will happen if you do *not* starting creating systems now? Two years will elapse whether or not you begin the process of system creation, so the only issue is whether you will be making significant progress toward the replication of your consulting practice or whether you will still be struggling with doing everything yourself in a nonreplicable manner.

In addition to systems, it is essential that organizations of any size—including an organization of one person—create a knowledge base. A knowledge base need not be a fancy database, but it does have to give you access to information in a comprehensive and easy-to-understand manner. One way to organize a knowledge base is to write a simple narrative for each client engagement. After every engagement, our consultants write a brief email or leave a voice mail describing the events of the day, what was particularly effective, any challenges they encountered, and appropriate next steps for the client. We use a contact management system that allows our client relations directors and consultants to know at a glance everything the client has done in the past. This has been extremely helpful in instances when the client asking for consulting services was careless and might have led us to make modification errors. In one case, we were asked to provide training to a large group of managers who had already had the very same training. The client contact shrugged it off, saying, "That's OK—give it to them again, they could use a double dose," not realizing how infuriated that roomful of people would have been if they had been forced to endure such a waste of time. Our own knowledge base knew what the client had, what the next step was, and how best to serve the client, even though the client didn't have that information and appeared to be indifferent to it.

Knowledge bases can also be situational, linked by key words. This is the way I assemble thousands of pieces of research and keep all that information available for reference within seconds. When I am asked a question about motivation or brain research, I can type those key words into the "find" box of a word-processing file, whereupon I will be directed to quotations from research studies I have accumulated over the years and continue to accumulate during each long airplane flight. When I answer a question with a specific citation, including the author, journal, and date, audiences are sometimes amazed either at my memory or my good luck to have had such information easily at hand. It is neither memory nor luck, but rather a laptop computer full of more research than I could possibly remember—research that is organized in a manner that makes information easy to retrieve.

The start of your knowledge base might be as easy as an engagement journal, with just a few paragraphs typed after every engagement day. You might consider the format of the "STAR report" in Figure 9.2. The "S" represents the *situation*. Describe it in sufficient detail to let a colleague understand where you were and what you were doing. The "T" represents the consulting *task* at hand. What you were asked to do? The "A" is for *actions,* and you should explain precisely what you did to accomplish the task and meet the client's needs. The "R" is for *results*. In this section of your engagement journal, explain precisely what results were or were not achieved. An individual engagement journal entry may seem little more than the ordinary details of your day, but a compilation of these entries over time can reveal some trends that would otherwise go unnoticed. For example, I have noticed that meetings with the same content, same agenda, and same participants are remarkably less productive in the late afternoon than they are in the morning. Though some clients insist that they are "just not morning people," my journal entries suggest that they are more energized, engaged, and productive at 7:30 in the morning than at their preferred meeting time of 4:00 in the afternoon. In other cases, the client insists that they wish to proceed at an advanced level of development—but the notes from multiple engagement journals suggest that I failed to include some fundamental steps because I unwisely assumed that every member of the client team was indeed at an advanced level of development. The inference to be drawn from my journal entries is not that I should argue with the client, but rather that I should build into every engagement some steps for pre-assessment and on-site needs analysis, so that every individual member of the client team receives the appropriate and necessary support.

In addition to creating written systems and developing and maintaining a knowledge base, consultants who wish to achieve their goal of replication must also integrate their knowledge so that new systems are built upon development knowledge, and the knowledge base is similarly informed by developing systems. Figure 9.3 suggests a means to conceptualize the need for integration. The process begins with a consideration of client needs, as described in the needs analysis referenced in Chapter 1. After each engagement, the consultant reflects on the task, actions, and results, all of which are recorded in the STAR report and a growing knowledge base, which can be in a form as informal as an engagement journal or as formal as a database. After accumulating a number of STAR reports, the consultant synthesizes the results, and begins to draw a series of inferences about the relationship between the consultant's actions and client results. Drawing on these inferences, the consultant is able to further refine the needs analysis and continue the process.

Without application of the integration process, the consultant will merely repeat the same services in response to the same perceived client need and,

Figure 9.2	Engagement Journal or "STAR" Report

Client: _____

Date: _____

Consultant: _____

SITUATION:

TASK:

ACTIONS:

RESULTS:

Additional Comments:

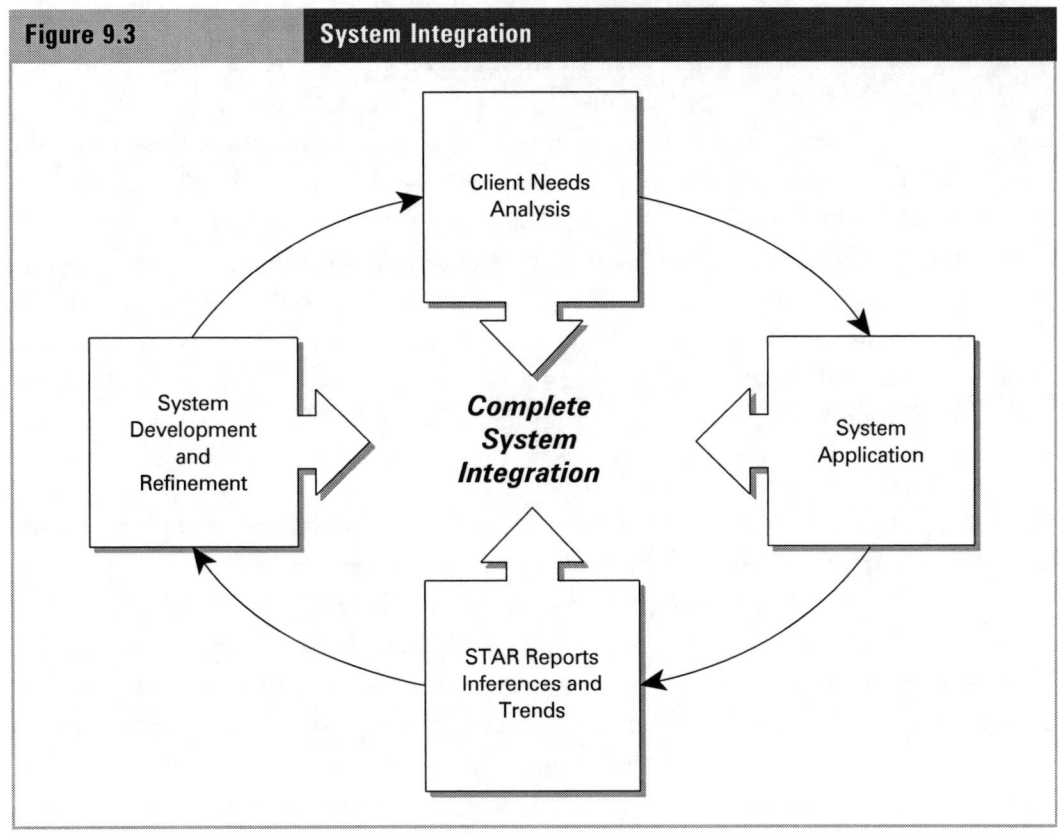

Figure 9.3   System Integration

in the blink of an eye, a partnership can turn to dust. "We've gone through all they have to offer," the client says, leaving the consultant perplexed as to why what she thought was a long-term relationship evaporated into mere pleasantries. Without effective integration and continuous reconsideration of client needs, consultant relationships will go through a cycle of identifying a need and either failing to meet it or merely meeting that need; in either case, the consultant fails to sustain the relationship. With effective integration, in contrast, the client's needs will be continuously refined, the delivery of services will be continuously improved, and the consultant's knowledge base will grow, creating a spiral of greater effectiveness and improved results.

Employee Ownership

The vast majority of knowledge-based organizations—law firms, accounting firms, medical practices, and consulting organizations—are owned by the employees. The vast majority of consulting firms are owned by the only employee, a sole practitioner. Most of the other firms are partnerships, closely held corporations, or limited liability companies. (There are notable exceptions, such as the organization formed when IBM purchased the consulting arm of PricewaterhouseCoopers, now known as IBM Business Consulting Services). For the most part, though, talent-based enterprises such as consulting organizations are employee-owned. The challenge is how best to structure employee ownership. The following are some alternatives that you may wish to consider, along with their relative advantages and disadvantages. The following paragraphs certainly do not constitute legal advice; they are only some brief observations about different ways to provide for employee ownership. If you are determined to be a sole proprietor, without any colleagues or employees and without any more formal form of business organization, then skip these paragraphs and proceed to the next section of the book.

General partnership. In the general partnership form of business organization, the partners own the company and have an agreement about how to share its profits and losses. Each partner bears general liability for the liabilities of the entire partnership. This means that if the partnership defaults on its rent or light bill, the landlord or electric company can seek payment from any or all of the individual general partners. General partnerships do not pay income taxes, as all income is distributed to the partners pursuant to the partnership agreement. This means that if the partnership retains some of its income to invest in equipment, finance accounts receivable, or save for the future, the partners will have taxable income but no cash income to pay the taxes. For example, if Mary and Bill are in a general partnership, split income evenly, and the partnership earns $200,000, then both Mary and Bill will have $100,000 of taxable income. If the partnership retains $40,000 of that income for operations or invests the same amount in real estate for a down payment on an office (neither savings nor investments are tax-deductible expenses), then each partner will receive half of the remaining $160,000 ($80,000 apiece) in cash income. Nevertheless, each partner's taxable income remains $100,000 and each partner must pay tax on that full amount. Finally, if Bill takes off for Tahiti, leaving a stack of unpaid bills behind, the creditors of the partnership will expect Mary to pay all those bills, not just her half. If either partner dies, becomes legally incompetent, declares bankruptcy, or resigns from the partnership, the partnership is automatically dissolved.

Limited partnership, limited liability company, and Subchapter S corporation. Each state has established specific organizational rules and criteria for limited partnerships (LPs) and limited liability companies (LLCs), and Canadian and European nations have similar forms of cooperative business organizations. Thus, some elements of these organizations are consistent despite the state-specific nature of many requirements. One key feature is that these organizations continue to exist even if one of the partners (or "members," as they are called in LLCs, or "shareholders," as they are called in Subchapter S corporations) dies or resigns. This is a significant advantage over the general partnership, as it avoids the chaos that can ensue if a single partner quits or dies. Another key feature is that these organizations, as the word *limited* implies, offer the owners a limitation of personal liability. In theory, creditors of an LP, LLC, or Sub S corporation can only attempt to seize the assets of the business organization; they cannot pursue the assets of the individual owners. This limitation may be more illusory than real, however, if major creditors—banks and landlords, for example—require the owners to sign personal guarantees of the debts of the LP, LLC, or S corporation. Like the general partnership, these entities pay no taxes, but distribute all of their income to their partners, members, or shareholders. Also like the general partnership, each individual is responsible for paying taxes on his or her share of the income, whether or not the individual has received cash income from the business.

Subchapter C corporation. This is the form of organization that most major businesses have adopted. The owners are called *shareholders.* In the case of public companies, the owners buy and sell stock in the public markets, such as the New York Stock Exchange. In the case of privately held companies, the owners buy and sell stock to willing buyers or sellers. Owners of Subchapter C corporations are typically not subject to liability for the business's debts unless, of course, the owners sign personal guarantees of company debt. C corporations continue in existence even if one of the owners dies or quits. C corporations are also permitted to provide a considerably wider range of employee benefits, including tax-deductible 401(k) plans and employee stock ownership plans, and a broader range of employer-paid medical benefits than are typically available in other forms of business organizations. However, C corporations pay their own income taxes. This results in double taxation of the same income. For example, if the C corporation earns $200,000, it will pay federal (and perhaps state) corporate income tax on that amount, then distribute what is left over to employees and owners, who must then also pay taxes on their personal income.

Which form to use? The decision as to which business form to adopt should be based on your personal objectives. I have been involved in sole proprietorships, limited liability companies, and Subchapter C corporations. When you are first starting in business, the sole proprietorship is easy. You file a single form, Schedule C (which you can download for free at www.irs.gov) as part of your personal federal income tax filing. As you expand, you may have people working for you. Before you hire them as employees, it might be wiser (and much easier) to engage these colleagues as independent contractors. As independent contractors, they own their own businesses, just as you do. They work for you under terms governed by a contract, and typically either party can discontinue the contract at any time. Independent contractors pay their own social security taxes and are responsible for all of their own benefits. Your obligation to them ends when you pay the fee specified in the contract.

What if one of these independent contractors becomes exceptionally valuable to you and you want to ensure a long-term relationship with that person? In this case, you may need to structure your organization in a way that allows the former independent contractors to share in the income, growth, and perhaps the ownership of your business. The form of business you choose to allow this should be selected carefully and with legal and accounting advice from professionals who specialize in small and growing professional practices such as yours.

One final note on sharing ownership with employees: Although I have a strong personal and philosophical commitment to employee ownership—I want my colleagues to "think like owners" because they really are owners—there are plenty of very smart people who disagree with me. These people note that the only people who really think like owners are the people who took risks with their own money and really do own the business, and that is a very small group of founders. Most employees, they argue, would much rather have an extra thousand dollars in their pocket than two thousand dollars' worth of ownership interest in your enterprise.

Moreover, the legal complications of employee ownership can be substantial. On the one hand, you want them to "think like owners," but what will you do when these "owners" look in the checkbook, see who is paid how much, and challenge your decision making? If the employees are genuinely owners, whether as partners, limited partners, members of a limited liability company, or shareholders, then they are legally entitled to a voice in the governance of the organization. As the founder—the person who put financial security on the line to build the enterprise, the person who worked very long hours for little or no compensation during the lean early years—are you really going to share ownership and authority with people who have made no such sacrifices? In my view, successful and growing organizations must answer that question in the affirmative. The votes of employees should be proportional to their ownership, something that happens most clearly in a corporate form of organization. If the founder retains a majority of the shares of the enterprise, the founder will be able to elect the board of directors. The directors hire and fire the officers and typically give daily operational authority to the executives. Over time, as employees accumulate more shares and a greater proportion of ownership, they will expect to have a greater voice in the affairs of the organization. Eventually, employees will have seats on the board of directors. Also, a shareholder can request at any time to see the books and records of the organization. Your fellow owners will know how much money the founder makes, how much stock she has, how many options she has, and every other item recorded in the minutes of the board of directors' meetings.

The prospect of prying employee eyes is one reason many entrepreneurs resist sharing ownership with the very people who helped make the enterprise a success. This reluctance is understandable. They remember the days of working three jobs, mowing the lawn and shoveling the snow in the apartment house, leaving at 3:00 a.m. for an engagement and returning home close to midnight, and repeating the process for seemingly endless days while missing innumerable family events. Perhaps some of these stories should be shared with employees, but after a while, employees will probably put the founder's tales in the same category as those told by their parents about walking to school in the snow, 12 months a year, uphill both ways. Just as great consultants must understand that it's not about them, but about the client, successful organizational leaders must create an appropriate balance between the organization and the employee. To be sure, the organization's history and the founder's personal commitment form part of the background of the firm that every employee should understand and appreciate. If they are to remain engaged and motivated, though, employees must know that their personal contributions to that work are significant, and that their rewards are fair. If employees cannot say with conviction, "My work is important, and I'm really good at what I do; I'm not rich, but I'm well paid—paid fairly for the hard work I do and the skills I bring to the job," then do not expect the compelling history of the founder's hard work in past years to motivate that employee.

Retaining Great People

Whether you are advising clients on employee motivation and retention or you are concerned with building your own organization, the issue of recruiting and retaining great people will frequently be at the forefront of your professional thoughts. Once you recognize that you cannot do it all alone, a considerable portion of your time will be focused on dealing with people issues. If, like me, you find this to be an exceptionally frustrating endeavor, either you must quickly find trusted colleagues to make these judgments—and then support them when they make the judgments you are unable or unwilling to make—or you must make the study of human motivation the most important consulting engagement you have ever undertaken. The *Harvard Business Review* published a classic series, "Motivating People," in a special edition (Stewart, 2003); Daniel Goleman and his colleagues assembled an impressive collection of evidence in landmark works titled *Working with Emotional Intelligence* (Goleman, 1998) and *Primal Leadership: Realizing the Power of Emotional Intelligence* (Goleman, Boyatzis & McKee, 2002). These researchers distinguish between genuine motivational elements of the relationship between employer and employee and what they called "hygiene factors," those things that are not necessarily linked to motivation, but the absence of which could seriously damage employee motivation and morale. In considering motivational factors across a wide variety of employers—businesses, nonprofit organizations, medical practices, military commands, and educational institutions—the researchers found that frequently discussed matters such as compensation and benefits are important, but not as motivators. Rather, the absence of appropriate financial security can be a significant *demotivator,* undermining employees' ability to recognize the factors that most influence their effectiveness. The most important motivational factors include the sense that employees are doing important work and that they are experiencing personal proficiency in their work. Unfortunately, the research on these matters, particularly the emotional needs of employees, is frequently misunderstood. Merely focusing on employees' emotional demands, without simultaneously creating strong performance demands, actually creates employee frustration, not satisfaction.

Figure 9.4 (originally presented in Reeves, 2004), suggests how appropriate performance demands intersect with a consideration of the emotional needs of colleagues. The upper right-hand quadrant is the province of the consultant and leader who misunderstands or misuses emotional intelligence research to supplant effective management with amateur therapy. The leader who persistently asks only, "What about *your* needs?" will train colleagues to reflexively ask, "What about *my* needs?" In the meanwhile, nobody is asking about the needs of the client. In the lower left-hand quadrant is the indifferent leader who neither imposes performance demands nor focuses on emotional needs. These leaders will perhaps not offend anyone during their short tenure, but they will not gain the respect of either colleagues or the stakeholders who demand effective performance. The lower right-hand quadrant is the domain of a great many consultants who are brought in to do the dirty work that employers are loathe to do themselves. With high performance demands and little respect for the emotional needs of the staff, they can create short-term results through restructuring, reengineering, downsizing, rightsizing, or any number of short-term initiatives. Nevertheless, people can work only so many seven-day weeks, we can endure a limited number of 18-hour days, and we can suffer a very limited number of destroyed relationships before we realize that Attila the Hun is not the best managerial role model. It is particularly ironic when the very consultants who exhort their clients to greater levels of sensitivity and emotional intelligence fail to heed their own advice and drive their colleagues and subordinates into the ground. They do not see that the consulting organization they have worked too hard to build is on the edge of the abyss until morale and effectiveness have been permanently damaged. In the upper right-hand quadrant are the effective leaders and consultants, people who have a high regard for the emotional needs of staff and simultaneously place a premium on great performance. Their colleagues feel successful not because of false affirmation, but from a genuine internal and external assessment of the quality and value of their work.

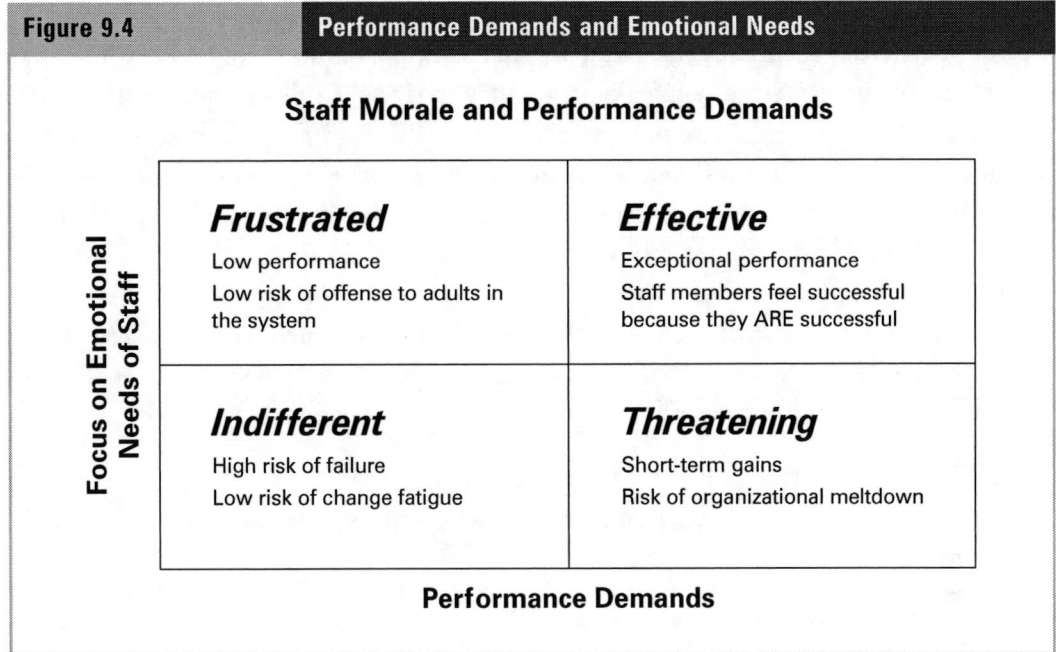

Figure 9.4   **Performance Demands and Emotional Needs**

Staff Morale and Performance Demands

Frustrated Low performance Low risk of offense to adults in the system	***Effective*** Exceptional performance Staff members feel successful because they ARE successful
Indifferent High risk of failure Low risk of change fatigue	***Threatening*** Short-term gains Risk of organizational meltdown

Focus on Emotional Needs of Staff (vertical axis label)

Performance Demands

Respect for Individual Needs

If you wish to build a talent-based organization, the most important strategy you can employ is to consider the individual needs of your colleagues. This is not only common sense, but also supported by a substantial body of research. The Gallup Organization's important study, documented in the book *First, Break All the Rules* (Buckingham & Coffman, 1999), concluded that common notions of fairness and consistency are mistaken. Although some people need daily affirmation, others need to be left alone, with only monthly check-ins. Although some people are paralyzed by negative feedback, others analyze it and use it to improve their performance. If you are going to build a consulting organization, the following are the most important words in this book: In a talent-based organization, individual freedom and personal consideration are the greatest employee benefits you can provide.

Here is a cautionary tale. One of the most effective leaders with whom I have ever worked was extraordinarily devoted to his employer and displayed exceptional personal loyalty to the CEO, his immediate boss. After more than seven years in a demanding and senior level position—after more than seven years of six- and seven-day weeks and fourteen-hour days, after more than seven years of taking multiple publicity bullets for the boss, completely reorganizing the headquarters, and achieving exceptional results—this superior leader made a simple request. He had developed an interest in overseas service, had taken private tutoring in a profoundly difficult language, and wanted to serve two days each quarter (eight days a year) overseas. This was his chance to make a difference and apply his expertise for those who needed him most. Many people in his situation could have sold their leave time for thousands of dollars a day, but this man wanted to give it away in the service of an impoverished nation. He wanted to use his own leave time, his own money, and his prodigious energy and, in the end, improve his own professional knowledge, all of which would have furthered the mission of his employer. Incredibly, his employer said "no." Hence, what might have been a long-lived, productive relationship is now in its declining days.

Although I have made a good many mistakes in my employee policies, here are some policies that might be worthy of emulation:

1. *Make no distinction between personal leave, medical leave, mental health leave, my-mother-is-sick leave, I'm-having-an-argument-with-my-teenager-but-don't-feel-like-discussing-it-right-now leave, and just-don't-feel-like-coming-in-to-work leave.* Your employees are grownups, and you should treat them as such. We start people with 15 days a year of leave and increase that amount to 27 days per year with longevity and good service. They can accumulate up to 60 days of paid leave—about three months of work—and they never need to bring in an excuse from a doctor or their mother. Leave is leave, and we trust them to use it wisely. Do not distinguish between maternal and paternal leave, or between leave for giving birth and leave for adopting a child. Do not distinguish between caring for a sick infant and caring for an ailing grandparent. Treat people as adults and they will return the favor by treating the employer as a trusted partner rather than an adversary. Even if they do not, you will know that you did the right thing.

2. *Use flex time for office colleagues.* Our office is open from 6:00 a.m. to 6:00 p.m., and employees can choose any eight working hours (with a required 30- to 60-minute lunch break) during that time. We just don't have arguments about who is a "morning person" and who prefers to come to work at 9:00. The issue is to get the job done, treat people as adults, and provide great service to our clients. We also make maximum use of technology, allowing people to work from the main office, a remote office, or a lakeside home. Soon we expect to be experimenting with international access to our network, so that employees can literally choose to work from anywhere in the world and continue to make valuable contributions to the team.

3. *Provide special consideration for traveling colleagues.* The life of travel is distinctly unglamorous. Those who travel are revenue generators for

any consulting organization, yet it is astounding how poorly they are often treated. In my more than two million miles of travel, I have been seated next to scores of consultants who are ready to leave their present employers over trivial matters. There are consultants who bring in a million dollars of revenue to their employer, take perhaps a fifth of that amount in personal income, yet are ready to quit because of a dispute over a $4.50 mini-bar tab, a $20 taxi fare, or a decision to use a $7-per-day navigation system to avoid being late to a client that generates hundreds of thousands of dollars in revenue. Tom Peters (Peters & Waterman, 1982; Peters & Austin, 1989) reminds us that retailing giant Nordstrom built a world-class retailing organization with only two rules: Don't chew gum and don't steal. Their organizational culture is replete with stories of employees who used their discretion to commit company funds in a manner that some might have regarded as unwise—personal deliveries, no-challenge refunds, and exceptional service on seemingly small items—but this is the stuff of which life-long customers are made. Men's Wearhouse is hardly a high-end retailer, but they have earned my loyalty and many thousands of dollars' worth of business because of the time I walked into their Cincinnati store at 8:45 p.m. in desperate need of a new suit; the job was done by half past nine, 30 minutes after they closed. There's also the time I ran into their south Denver store, on the way to the airport, after noticing that my pants had split; within minutes, I was back on my way to the airport. I think that my company has some life-long customers because we have given our employees discretion to provide great service and make spot decisions. To be sure, these are not always the decisions I would have made, but they are invariably decisions based on the best judgment of the people we have hired to make them.

4. *Make common cause with employees against the rising cost of health care.* We cannot control the rising cost of health care or the decreasing likelihood that insurance companies will reimburse employees for medical expenses. We can, however, do some rational and logical things to make it clear that employees and employers are on the same side of the table. At the very least, every employer should have a cafeteria benefits plan, allowing employees to make pretax deductions from their income to pay for nonreimbursed medical expenses. Without such a plan, an employee needs to make $125 to $150 just to pay for $100 of nonreimbursable medical expenses. With a cafeteria plan, the full $150 of income can be applied toward medical expenses, as well as expenses commonly not addressed by medical care plans, such as dental and eye care and many therapeutic, laboratory, and pharmaceutical expenses. In addition, cafeteria benefit plans can be used to pay for care for children and adults in need of day care or other assistance. In our case, we recently changed insurance carriers, but we know that the new carrier will leave our employees (ranging in age from 18 to 60) with a wide range of health care costs that are not covered. Therefore, we passed along all of the savings from the insurance

company switch—about $1,000 per employee—to our employees. Specifically, we make a $1,000-per-year contribution to each employee's cafeteria benefits plan. For one employee, who incurs about $80 in unreimbursed lab fees and office visits per month, the contribution will prevent excessive out-of-pocket disbursements. For other employees who remain healthy and have no need of medical care, the additional $1,000 comes back each year in cash as taxable income. Finally, for employees who do not take advantage of our health care plan, we provide a cash supplement in the amount we would otherwise have spent on their health insurance—about $2,400 per year per employee. Whatever the case, it is clear that when our employees confront the rising cost of health care, they will know that we are on their side.

5. Recognize learning as a benefit, not a cost. The best employees find learning an opportunity, not an obligation. We give employees $50 certificates to buy any book or tape they want, asking only that they tell us about what they learned. We give top-level employees subscriptions to www.Audible.com, a great source of unabridged recorded books on a variety of sources. I don't care if they select Homer's *Odyssey* or Daniel Goleman's *Primal Leadership*—I have downloaded and listened to both. The key is that great people want to learn and great employers nurture that ambition. We support continuing education, including helping employees earn advanced degrees and professional certifications. The risk in this strategy is that employees may learn so much that they become valuable to another employer and leave us; this happened when we helped a junior financial employee to study for and earn his Certified Public Accountant designation. Another employee earned his doctorate and qualified for a position with an employer that doubled the salary we paid. For each of these examples, however, there are many more employees from whom we have earned long-term loyalty and terrific performance.

In the next chapter, we acknowledge that the imperatives of providing great service and building a successful organization are not always compatible with the needs of family, friends, and personal sustenance. Although I make no pretense that anyone can have it all, I do believe that one can bounce back from an excessive devotion to professional interests, recognize error, learn from mistakes, and pursue one's best interests both at home and at work.

Synthesis: Having a Life, Serving Clients, and Building an Organization

The Myth of Balance

Organizational Disciplines

Personal Disciplines

Consulting can be an exciting, creative, entrepreneurial, and intense profession. Intensity, however, is a two-sided coin, with the shiny side reflecting the best days of engagement in our work, and the dull side masking the sacrifices we make. Because consulting is a time-intensive profession, and because time is a fixed quantity for everyone, the greatest commitment that consultants make—time with clients—is also their greatest sacrifice—time with family, friends, and ourselves.

In the following pages, I acknowledge my own errors in managing time and also offer some suggestions for how you can devote the energy your consulting practice requires and nevertheless maintain some boundaries around the time required for personal renewal.

The Myth of Balance

I have made a number of intemperate comments in my communications with my colleagues at the end of a long day. Some of those comments are remembered fondly, including the time I greeted Larry Ainsworth at two in the morning in the Knoxville, Tennessee, airport with the words, "Welcome to the glamorous world of consulting." Other comments have more of an edge to them. My colleagues remember them, but not always so fondly. Just last week I confessed to being tired on a Tuesday when Monday began at 3:30 a.m. in Boston, took me to Pennsylvania for an afternoon keynote presentation, then on a flight to Washington, D.C., and at last to Denver, where I arrived at my hotel precisely 24 hours after I had awakened. Before my complaints of fatigue received any sympathy, however, I was reminded of another aphorism I had coined when the roles were reversed. "I thought you said 'sleep is for wimps,'" Tony reminded me. When I encourage my colleagues to take a balanced approach to life, their rejoinder is an immediate and pointed reminder of my statement that "Sure I'm balanced—excessive in all things."

Despite the cynicism and fatigue that might have gotten the better of me when I uttered those words, there is a ring of truth to them. I ride the rails and the airways sitting next to people who regularly spend four to five days a week, 48 to 50 weeks every year, away from home—that's 192 to 250 nights away from family and loved ones, from hobbies and diversions, from school plays and track meets, from first recitals and graduations—every single year. At my firm, where we regard ourselves as a very family-friendly organization, we annually celebrate consultants who have 100 or more paid engagement days (the vast majority of which require out-of-town travel) by giving the "Century Club" recognition, which comes with perks, rewards, vacation, and economic incentives. Although my travel schedule has been curtailed in the past few years, I nevertheless routinely put in 100 days on the road every year. To this day, long after I could have reduced my schedule more significantly, I often hear a ten-year-old say, "You sure have been gone a lot lately."

The Internet is no longer a new technology, and teleconference and videoconference technology have been around for more than two decades, but person-to-person contact remains the primary method by which consulting services are delivered, particularly during the relationship-building and business-development phases of the engagement. I know consultants who had the fantasy that they could grow their businesses over the Internet; there is a continuing stream of books promising that you can "work naked" (Froggatt, 2001), or at least placidly type away at the keyboard in your bathrobe, while making every play date, carpool assignment, and Little League game. The *Harvard Business Review* set off a firestorm of controversy with the article that coined the term "the Mommy track" (Schwartz, 1989), suggesting that employees (most typically women) should be able to get off the fast track for five to seven years, have a more reasonable schedule, raise a family, and then rejoin the workforce later. The howls in the subsequent letters to the editor could be heard from coast to coast. "Why just Mommy? Why not Daddy? Why should either gender have to sacrifice job for family? Why not have a more humane work schedule for everybody? Why don't employees understand that customers, shareholders, colleagues, and clients do not care about their personal lives?"

This is a place not for social commentary, but for reality. So here are the facts. First, in most consulting enterprises, you will spend a great deal of time, including uncompensated time, developing new client business. You will give presentations early in the morning and late in the evening, meet with clients at times that are convenient for them rather than for you, and get an extraordinary amount of work done on seemingly impossible deadlines. After all, if the clients could do this work without your assistance, they would. You have the engagement precisely because you can do the impossible, achieving what the clients' own employees could not or would not.

Second, time allocation is a zero-sum game in which every hour you choose to spend on a client matter is an hour you will not spend with family, friends, becoming healthier, reading the Great Books, or attending a local school board meeting.

Third, your ability to exercise choice in how you spend your time—even though those choices may be the subject of a lot of second-guessing, complaining, and self-flagellation—is a true privilege that many other occupations do not provide. Attorneys are subject to the schedule demands of judges. Retail managers are subject to the seasons, rarely having a private moment between mid-November and the end of the calendar year. Accountants notoriously work nonstop from January through the April 15 tax deadline. These executives and professionals knew when they accepted their positions that their schedules were not their own. Consultants, by contrast, have the ability to say "no" to any engagement, any meeting, and any deadline. Of course, they are also potentially saying "no" to their paychecks and client base. Still, our ability to exercise that choice is something we should cherish and not bemoan.

Fourth, if you want more family time, then schedule it—now. My calendar is typically set at least a year in advance. Therefore, the only way I can have family vacations is to schedule them at least a year in advance. Airlines typically allow reservations for free tickets using frequent flier miles about 330 days in advance of travel. By hitting that deadline religiously, I not only make use of my frequent flier miles, but also schedule family vacation time far in advance and prevent client obligations from stepping on family commitments. Moreover, when my family can see vacations coming half a year or a year in the future, it can somewhat relieve the sting of my absences that give us the ability to take those vacations.

Let us maintain no illusions here, though. For every play performance, concert, recital, and game I have attended, I have missed a dozen. For each time I was there for a perfect moment of parental bonding, there were an equal number of faceless telephone conversations with a weak and preoccupied "I love you" at the other end of the line. I built my company because I love what I do and believe it is important work, but I make no pretense that it has not taken a toll on my family. My father turned down promotions and economic incentives in order to remain in a smaller town and, to a very large extent, be present for his children. I grew up in a home that had formal family dinners five nights a week, and less formal but nevertheless cohesive and conversation-filled family dinners the other two nights of the week. We strive to have a single family dinner each week and, as the children grow older, even those dinners are hurried and disjointed affairs. This is the life I have chosen, and I do not regret it. Nevertheless, I will not offer the reader any pabulum that suggests that you can "have it all" by simultaneously committing the same hour to family and work. You will make choices, and you must be thankful for the ability to make them.

Organizational Disciplines

When you are a consultant, time is literally money. Although many organizations do not realize it, the same equation is true for them, and their expenditures of time are profligate in the extreme. They hold two-hour meetings with neither agendas nor meaningful resolutions. They undertake projects with fuzzy goals and meaningless milestones. They make interoffice presumptions of understanding that are undocumented, unstated, and completely inaccurate. They have pathologically dysfunctional communication patterns in which every meeting is followed by a "real" meeting in the parking lot, coffee shop, or restroom. Fortunately, the consultant has the opportunity to make a lasting impact on the client organization by imposing order amidst organizational chaos. Here are some rules of engagement that effective consultants should require from their colleagues and their clients.

Facts

Great consultants never wing it. They never assume. They never engage in guesswork. Although some clients may marvel at the intuitive insight of a particularly effective consultant, intuition is not magic, but rather the ability to make nonobvious connections of apparently unrelated facts. The greatest warning sign of trouble for any consulting engagement is when the client is unwilling or unable (far more likely the former than the latter) to share essential facts that will allow the consultant to perform an effective needs analysis. Because most effective consulting engagements are premised on the creation of organizational change, there are always and inevitably resisters to those changes within the organization. Resisters to change have a vast repertoire of ways to subvert the efforts of outside consultants and any leadership change initiative, but one of the easiest and most effective arrows in their quiver is to make the consultant look like a fool in a public meeting because the consultant didn't have essential pieces of information. When—not if—you confront these resisters, you need to be able to say with certainty, "Your facts are wrong; my facts are right; these recommendations are in the best interest of your organization."

Facts are best gathered by asking deliberately naïve questions. Even when you and your colleagues are not expert in a field, you can politely but persistently ask questions during a needs analysis interview after every client assertion. When the client says, "Our staff morale is great," "We need to improve communication," "Our quality is superior," "Our real problems are only in this division, department, facility, person, etc.," or any other similar assertion, great consultants ask—politely but persistently—questions such as:

- How have you measured this? I'd really be interested in seeing as much data as you have on this.

- What other data do we have that is similar to or different from these measurements?

- What would the data need to look like for you to regard it as successful? How was that definition of *success* determined?

- If we don't have extensive data on this, please help me understand how you arrived at your conclusion. You're an expert in this area and I'm not— could you walk me through your thought process on this?

- What other outside advice have you received on this matter? Did they publish written reports? I'm a sponge for this sort of thing—please give me as much as you have.

When your company has many different consultants involved in a project, it will be necessary for you to provide an easy way to give everyone in the organization who has a need to know access to all the accumulated information on these clients. We use a Web-based system in which our consultants have password-protected access to a Web site that has every detail of every engagement with every client. Each state or country is a separate folder. Within each folder are lists of clients. Within each client list is a set of documents for each engagement. If you want to know what presentation we provided to Costa Mesa, California, three years ago, you just click the "California" folder and then the "Costa Mesa" folder and in a matter of minutes, you can see all that we have done with that particular client.

One of the best ways to start any meeting is to say, "I know I have a lot to learn, but here is what I've already learned about you . . . ." This immediately distinguishes you from the legions of consultants who think that every engagement is about them and not about the client. It shows that you took the time and interest to learn about the local context. It shows that you are not the officious expert with an agenda, but a fellow learner willing to consider the client as a singularity that deserves individual attention.

Finally, the commitment to facts allows you to gently but firmly enforce the "no guessing" rule suggested by Khalsa (1999). His book and audio program contain a wealth of practical information that every consultant should heed.

Meetings

The price of a meeting is an agenda, with a clear statement of desired results as well as meaningful and enforced times for beginning and ending. Some of the most effective meetings I have ever attended were concluded within a very few minutes by a forceful leader, convener, or outside consultant who said, "We appear to have accomplished all we can as a group, so let's use our time more wisely outside of this meeting." Figure 10.1 provides some useful guidelines for effective meetings. Consider distributing this in advance of your next meeting or making it an appendix to any meetings you are expected to convene as an external consultant. Of course, you will have to practice what you preach, so the days of meetings as an entertaining diversion from productive work will at last come to an end. Figure 10.2 provides a simplified example of an agenda, along with the expectations and contributions you have of meeting participants. If you cannot complete the part of the form about "expected contributions" of a participant, then why in the world would you ask that person to waste time attending your meeting?

Figure 10.1	Meeting Guidelines

1. **Meetings capitalize on the collective wisdom of a group.** The only reason we have meetings is that we are convinced a better decision will be made collectively than individually. Come to this meeting only if you are prepared to participate in a better collective decision.

2. **Meetings are voluntary.** If your time will be better invested doing something else, then do that. You are not evaluated based on meeting attendance; you are evaluated based on personal effectiveness in achieving individual and organizational goals.

3. **Meetings are "announcement-free zones."** Any announcements must be made by voice mail or email. We do not waste precious meeting time for announcements. Before you say the words, "I just wanted to share . . . ," stifle the impulse and send us a message. Before you deliver a PowerPoint presentation of something that everyone has already read, turn off the computer and say, "I realize you are already familiar with this information, so let's focus on the following action items . . . ." In brief, stop lecturing and listen.

4. **Do your homework.** If there are readings or analyses that you must complete before the meeting in order to make a meaningful contribution, then either do so or decline the invitation to the meeting. Nobody has time for you to do your homework while we wait.

5. **Start and end on time.** Every book ever written on meeting management says this, but too many meetings start late while everyone waits patiently for the conference call system to work; for the 20-year veteran technology expert to figure out the videoconference or teleconference system, or, for that matter, how to use the "hold" button; or for the distinguished leader to walk into the room. Disciplined organizations start meetings on time. If the leader is not there, someone else starts the meeting, confident in the knowledge that such an action elevates organizational effectiveness over personal ego.

Figure 10.2	Agenda

Date: _____

Start: _____

End: _____

Participants:

Name	Role	Expected Contribution

(continues)

Figure 10.2 (Continued)	**Agenda**

Purpose:

By the end of this meeting, we will:

_____

_____

Background:

Before the meeting, each participant will read and review:

_____

_____

Decisions:

1. _____

2. _____

3. _____

4. _____

Definition of Results

Effective organizations know the results they want to achieve and express them in quantitative terms. Whether those results are expressed in terms of sales, net profit, customer satisfaction, employee engagement, student achievement, or any other objective, results are not worthy of the name if they are not measurable. Consultants set themselves up for failure on a regular basis when they accept ambiguity in the definition of results. Rather than taking the time to engage in measurement of results, unsuccessful and impatient consultants engage in the self-delusion facilitated by popularity ratings. Sounding like Sally Fields accepting an Academy award ("You like me! You really like me!"), they substitute the smile sheets—evaluations of the quality of their presentations—for results. In the short term, the smile sheets assuage the feelings of both consultant and client. If your objective is to build long-term relationships, however, it is essential that you go beyond the smile sheets and achieve measurable results that have been agreed upon in advance. Because organizational results depend on a variety of factors beyond the work of consultants, it is essential not only that you define what the word *results* means, but also that you codify in writing the specific actions the client and the consultant will take.

Time Management

Chapter 6 elaborated on the need for a Daily Prioritized Task List, the single most important tool in effective time management for consultants (and members of any organization). Effective consultants challenge their clients rather than flatter them. Great consultants demand of themselves, their colleagues, and their clients greater focus and productivity than any of them had believed possible. To ensure that the organizational discipline of time management operates continuously, the best consultants ask these questions on a regular basis:

- What are your top six tasks in priority order today?
- When was the last time you updated your DPTL?
- How many of the tasks that you have listed can be accomplished in less than 45 minutes?
- How many of the tasks that you have listed can be accomplished only by you?

You cannot expect clients to respond to these questions if you cannot respond to them as well. For me, time management is a daily, almost an hourly, struggle. I am diverted, tempted, and swayed by every time-wasting bad habit in the world. I'm a CNN junkie when I know I have a chapter or article to finish; there is a short story, poem, or novel that entices me when I have more than 100 emails to answer; there is a great new ethnic restaurant with luxurious service that could occupy my evening when the smart thing to do would be room service with soup and salad. I have given up neither CNN, short stories, poems, novels, nor ethnic food, but I do put almost everything I do on my list, and give myself the psychic and personal rewards that I enjoy in a sequence that makes sense. I still enjoy, as I did this weekend, wonderfully spontaneous and unplanned hours with my family. We go to the park, museum, or seashore at the drop of a hat, with no entries on the calendar and no advance planning required. For each spontaneous hour, though, there are many more that are planned in detail. John Wooden, one of the greatest collegiate basketball coaches of all time, devoted many more hours to planning each practice than his players spent on the court. Great consultants do not enter engagements without thoughtful planning and minute-to-minute schedules. My greatest failures as a consultant have been born of assumptions, thinking that the details would take care of themselves.

You might wonder why these very personal activities of time management fall under "organizational discipline" rather than personal requirements. The answer is simple: Whether your organization consists of two people or two thousand, time management techniques, such as prioritized task lists, work best when everyone in the organization uses them. Inconsistent application of this discipline leads inevitably to contention and, in every sense of the term, disorganization. There are many areas in which your colleagues can express their individuality—art on the wall, pictures of kids in the cubicle, or even voice-mail greetings. Time management is the consulting organization's equivalent of handwashing for a restaurant employee: we love creativity in the menu; we loathe creativity in hygiene.

Civility

In one of the more provocative articles ever published in the otherwise staid *Harvard Business Review* (Sutton, 2004), the editors asked leading researchers and executives to suggest their most compelling ideas for organizational excellence in the twenty-first century. The arresting phrase that jumped from the pages of this august academic journal was the suggestion that organizations adopt the "no jackasses" rule. This was not merely the scatological musing of an author who had had a bad day, but a reflection of the preponderance of scientific evidence about group processes and organizational effectiveness. For example, Dr. Herbert Benson, author of the landmark book *The Relaxation Response* (Benson & Klipper, 1975) and the immensely practical volume *The Breakout Principle* (Benson & Proctor, 2003), noted that although conflict is inevitable in organizations, and though conflict is in fact an essential part of the creative process, the advantages of creativity are nullified when the norms of interpersonal conflict give way to uncivil behavior. Benson, a medical doctor and researcher, described the Grating Paradox as follows: "In an organization, intense but cordial disagreement is necessary to product innovation, enhanced productivity, worker satisfaction—and lasting agreement" (p. 153).

Disagreement is necessary for agreement? Precisely. We cannot choose to avoid disagreement, but only to choose where (and sometimes how) it will take place. Either disagreement takes place in the open, in the fresh air and safe environment of an effective team, or disagreement takes place in the sequestered atmosphere of the hushed water-cooler or parking-lot discussion. We cannot choose to avoid disagreement; we *can* choose whether the disagreements are constructive and civil or destructive and organizationally toxic. As a consultant who possesses a high degree of expertise in your field, and as a consultant who will interact with high-level clients who also possess a great deal of expertise in their domains, the civility mandate is particularly imperative. In Benson's words, "It is essential to emphasize the 'cordiality' qualification of the above definition. This caveat becomes especially important when members are highly accomplished in their respective fields and probably possess an extra measure of self-confidence, if not arrogance" (p. 153).

My own experiences as a consultant invariably color my views on this subject. I must acknowledge that while I take the imperative of civility seriously,

I have failed to maintain it with complete fidelity. For the past 30 years I have held leadership positions of one degree or another, initially as a platoon leader and battery commander in the United States Army, and later as the president of a consulting organization that works in all 50 states and throughout the world. My worst days as a leader were those in which I lost my temper, or worse yet, maintained my cool but calmly eviscerated the ideas, proposals, and sense of personal worth of a colleague. This is exceedingly embarrassing to admit, but it is the truth. The damage inflicted by incivility is incalculable, and has long-lasting impact throughout the organization. Just as a single schoolyard bully can poison the atmosphere of a playground or entire neighborhood, so also a single negative person—the sort who is unremittingly critical, unwilling and unable to support the creative brainstorms of colleagues, and behaves more like an attack dog than a leader—can devastate an organization for years.

The *American Behavioral Scientist* (Cameron & Caza, 2004) suggests that effective organizations maintain a "P/N Ratio"—a measurement of positive and negative comments—that reflects at least five times more positive comments than negative comments. Consider a single case in which you have been asked for assistance, whether as part of a formal consulting engagement, as an informal advisor, or as a family friend. Mentally review your telephone conversations, emails, and discussions about the matter. What was the ratio of positive to negative comments? Certainly it was not 5:1; in fact, it might have been 1:5—five times as many negative comments as positive, with the accolades only grudgingly admitted after a litany of complaints.

Unfortunately, many consultants thrive on negativity, as it appears to be an invitation for their services. After all, if there were no problems, the client would not need a consultant. A contrary view, and one much more aligned with long-term organizational success, is to conduct a "treasure hunt" (Reeves, 2002b) in which analysis of data and decisions begins with a focus on what is most effective. When you are asked to address a problem, focus first on the successes, including the "buried treasure" that the clients did not know they had:

> "I know that you are disappointed in company-wide sales, but Region III experienced a jump last quarter. Why were you so effective there?"

> "I know that fifth-grade math scores are down, but Mr. McArthur's class experienced great gains in problem-solving scores. Why were you so effective there?"

> "I know that customer satisfaction is lower than you want, but the stores in Toledo and Topeka had significantly higher scores in customer satisfaction. Why were you so effective there?"

The treasure-hunt mentality is not just about identifying and solving problems; rather, it's about identifying strengths and building on those strengths.

As Buckingham and Clifton (2001) suggested, it is faster and easier for individuals and organizations to build on their strengths than to compensate for weaknesses. As psychologist Martin Seligman (1998) has noted, the positive and optimistic frame of mind is not merely the reflection of a sunny disposition, but the result of an explicit choice. Individuals and organizations are healthier when we choose optimism and reject cynicism.

Personal Disciplines

Covet Time

We are admonished in many religious traditions not to "covet." The *Oxford English Dictionary* suggests the pejorative contexts in which the term is typically encountered, nearly equating it to thievery. To *covet, Oxford* suggests, is to "yearn to possess something belonging to someone else." In the context of time, however, the negative implication is inapt. Your time belongs to you, and your failure to covet it will result in the squandering of this valuable resource. The personal discipline of coveting time requires more than merely conducting meetings responsibly (and insisting that others do so), maintaining a Daily Prioritized Task List (and insisting that others do so), and establishing and meeting commitments (and insisting to the point of fanaticism that others do so). Coveting time is a deeply personal discipline in which we must deeply value each day, hour, and minute. Perhaps it sounds like a cliché to suggest the question, "What would you do if you knew you only had six months to live?" If the answer is anything other than what you are doing right now, it is well past time for a serious reassessment of priorities. The great organist, César Franck (1822–1890) died while at the console of the organ in the Cathedral of Notre Dame in Paris. Perhaps you have family members or friends whose lives ended precisely as they might have wished, after a lifetime of pursuing their heart's desire and with a deep sense of fulfillment. It is also very likely, though, that you know of people whose deaths happened far too early, their lives marked by regret as to tasks unfulfilled and relationships unhealed.

When we adopt the personal discipline of coveting time, we acknowledge every moment, including those devoted to uninterrupted relaxation, the joy of watching children in a park, the silent moments of hand-holding with a spouse, or the sheer pleasure of reading not for speed and content, but for the sensuous pleasure of the book in hand, the expressive word on the page, challenging thoughts expressed in chapters rather than sound bites. When we covet time, each of these golden moments is as important as our greatest professional triumphs, whether those consisted of a brilliant presentation before a board of directors, a standing ovation from an audience, or the completion of a major project. When we covet time, we are appropriately impatient and intolerant of those who waste our time, knowing that for each minute wasted, there is a wonderful alternative to that waste in which we can indulge our personal and professional passions. When we covet time, we envision watching children we love in a school play, giving a music recital, making an academic presentation, at a skateboard park, on a camping trip, or a thousand other activities and we ask, "Would I rather be doing what I am right now, or would I rather be watching kids I love doing what they love?" This blunt question does not always mean that I stop in mid-presentation and head home in time to see the school play, but the question does help to make me shorten meetings, focus discussions, and otherwise respect my own time and that of my clients. Here are just a few of the ways in which I covet time:

- *I will not stand idly in lines.* Although today's airline security rules certainly create many opportunities for me to waste hours—years in my case—of time standing in line and despairing of the ineptness of airlines and security personnel, I either read or listen to books on tape whenever I am forced to stand in a line. It doesn't make any difference whether the wait is five minutes or two hours, I make use of every second. Whether the line is at Starbucks, the grocery store, the pharmacy, the subway, or the airport, I always have something to read in my pocket. It may look odd for a rumpled *New York Times Book Review* section, W. Somerset Maugham short-story collection, Jane Smiley novel, or collection of essays from Harper's to appear from my coat pocket, but lines mean that I almost always find time to read these wonderful diversions—a sheer pleasure for somebody whose time is often consumed by the demands of a nonfiction life and hundreds of emails. While others in line are whining, I am reading or listening, coveting every moment of time.

- *I will excuse myself from pointless meetings.* It is, I admit, unseemly to remain in a meeting and blatantly answer email while purporting to gain points for attendance. It is more honest to ask the simple question, "Is there anything else I can contribute to this meeting?" The answer will rarely be a straightforward "no"; usually it's a shocked silence. The polite thing to do is to offer a face-saving gesture, such as, "I know you're very busy and have a great deal of work to do, so I'll put my ideas in writing and forward them to all of you." You graduated from putting in face time a long time ago. Be nice, be smart, covet your time, rise from your chair, and leave the meeting.

- *I will lavish time on people who respect my time.* In addition to avoiding people who waste time, I actively seek and engage those who use my time well. The right to "just check in" or "see how you are doing" is earned by those who respect my time as if it were their own.

Be Appropriately Antisocial

I can count on a very few fingers the number of client dinners I have attended in the past ten years. I have never—not once—played golf with a client. I have never—not once—gone to a bar, gone dancing, or attended a theatrical event with a client. I'm not an antisocial person, but I have an acute understanding of my capabilities and my limitations. Among my many limitations is the inability to feign interest when I have none. I have many friends who enjoy golf and use their time on the links to further their business interests. May they find their time communing with crew-cut greens and personal frustration fruitful. Their skills in the game of golf, as well as the personal traits of forbearance and eye-hand coordination, surely outstrip mine. Therefore, I concede the field to them. I am more than happy to meet with a client for breakfast, with an agenda focused on a clear objective and a clear ending time, typically established by the client's own starting time for another presentation at about 8:30 a.m. I am also very happy to do a "calorie-free" lunch in which we dispense with the interruptions of menus, selections, and eating to focus on the client's most important needs. What I almost never do, however, is to engage in a dinner that is almost invariably laden with too much food and alcohol and devoid of essential business content.

Thank Clients and Colleagues

As this chapter is being composed, I am sitting next to that rarest of individuals, a man who takes pen in hand and devotes a cross-country trip to composing personalized thank-you notes to family, friends, and clients. I perform this ritual each week. My handwriting is imperfect and my expressions less eloquent than Hallmark might contrive, but each word is chosen for the individual to whom it is addressed. The stationery is not flashy, but it is personalized with my home address. The notes are not huge, but within the space of a four-inch by four-inch space, I can say "Thank you" for the kindness that clients and colleagues extend to me each day of my professional life. There may be some people who would say, "Forget the sentiment—I'd rather have cold cash," but there are certainly many more who say, "I've been doing this job for decades and you are the first person to thank me."

Record Your Ideas

Even if you pen only a few sentences, your reflections on the day have value. What is particularly interesting is the *Journal 10+* (Koshiyama, 2003) in which you record your observations for each day of the year in a row across each page, with each row representing a different year. This format forces the journalist to compare prejudice to reality. The events that we were certain were singularities are, in fact, repetitive. The feelings that we wish to attribute to circumstance or interactions with others are, in fact, reflective of consistent traits of our being. I do not write for the ages, as my musings are hardly the Confessions of St. Augustine. Rather, I just write to better understand myself and the world of which I am a very small part. When I review my ideas a few times each year, I am invariably astonished at the notions that virtually leap from the page with their repetition and zeal. Because the same ideas seemed fragmentary and isolated as I recorded them, I routinely ignored them. Now, noticing that the same theme emerged again and again over time, I cannot ignore these repetitive imperatives.

Call Mom

In the years since cell-phone use has become ubiquitous, a habit of macho turf-marking has arisen, meaning that loud, overbearing, and nearly dictatorial conversations take place on airplanes and in airport clubs, among many other places. "My client, my subordinate, my boss," these obnoxious and loud exchanges seem to claim, "are more important than yours." Enter Mom. I call my mother every Friday. She is in her eighties and still going to the gym every day, driving her friends to appointments, volunteering in her community, and helping the "old" people, a group that surely does not include herself. Besides the Friday call, when I have time while changing concourses or boarding an airplane in my travels, I also make several calls just to give a weather report from that part of the world. After these calls, a surprising number of people have said to me, "I just called my mom too—thanks for reminding me." My mother takes a good deal of satisfaction from inducing maternal guilt not only in me but also in legions of unknown travelers who, after hearing only half of a conversation, are compelled to call their mothers. Thanks, Mom—talk with you on Friday.

CHAPTER 11

Epilogue: What I Wish I Had Known When I Started Consulting

This is the eleventh chapter in a ten-chapter book. I added it because my colleagues at the Center for Performance Assessment offered 20 simple but valuable insights. I simply asked them: "What do you know now that you wish you had known when you started in our profession?"

Here is a distillation of their responses.

1. Pre-engagement planning is absolutely essential if you want to ensure that client expectations are met and to avoid very unpleasant surprises. Make sure that you talk to *all* the decision makers. Try to determine underlying agendas by "reading between the lines" during the call(s) you have with client representatives prior to the engagement. Being unaware of these may sabotage your efforts.

2. Acknowledge publicly the hard work the clients have already done. The recognition you afford them will come back to you tenfold in their support of the work you have been brought in to do.

3. Client relationships are best built by making each client feel that it is your only client. Be responsive to their wishes, make recommendations when asked, listen carefully, be respectful, and follow up on all promises you make before, during, and after the presentation. Above all, strive to serve the client's agenda while fulfilling your responsibility to deliver your firm's message, which your firm is paying you to deliver to the best of your ability. Accomplish all the objectives of that particular seminar within the time frame you are given.

4. Travel—welcome to the glamorous world of consulting! There's really only one rule here. Prepare early, be detail oriented, and be ever ready to "go with the flow" when you miss your flight connection, your hotel room is noisy, the driving directions you have been given are incorrect, or any number of other challenges arise. Smile, relax, and treat all travel-related employees (airlines, hotel, and car rental, among others) as you would like to be treated.

5. When dealing with upset clients, listen, acknowledge their distress or displeasure, and do everything you can, without sacrificing your integrity or putting the firm in an awkward situation, to rectify the perceived wrongs. Maintain as much grace under pressure as you can, and remember that you represent the firm best by the character you display. Remind yourself, "This too shall pass," because it will.

6. When traveling, be sure you are always aware of your layover time! You might think it's 1:00 in Los Angeles, but forget that it's 3:00 in Chicago where you are changing planes. When you are going nonstop, it is easy to get time zones confused. If you do, you may hear your name being mispronounced over the airport loudspeaker, and find yourself running from the Red Carpet Room, if you are really lucky, to the last gate in the terminal.

7. Don't ask the client to make copies for you on the morning of a presentation. That's what copy shops are for.

8. Make sure you get on the right flight to the right city; otherwise, you might miss your connection. It's very common to have two different flights going to Chicago within a few gates of each other. Always check flight number and destination. (Doug's note: I always heard the comment from flight attendants saying, "If this city is not your final destination, now would be an ideal time to leave the aircraft," and thought, "What sort of idiot would be on the wrong airplane?" Then I found myself sitting in my usual seat aboard what I thought was a flight to Anchorage, Alaska, and heard the announcement, "If Hong Kong is not your final destination, now would be an ideal time to leave the aircraft." I came within minutes of missing my flight and having a very, very long detour. Do not depend on the airlines and their computers to overcome human error—including your own.

9. Avoid booking the last flight into or out of a particular location. If there is a cancellation, this leaves you with almost no options.

10. Print out directions and maps to hotel and client locations from a trusted computerized source, such as Yahoo Directions or MapQuest. Never rely solely on client directions.

11. Know your firm's research cold. Clients sometimes ask detailed questions about the associated research for which we are best known, and I need to know every detail of each study.

12. Have documentation of successful work by clients, including videotapes of their work. This doesn't have to be fancy. The key is to make it clear that real people have been through the same process before.

13. Analyze mock series of client data sets before you deal with an actual client. I wish I'd had a crash course on the specific sorts of data the client used before I was required to deal with a client's data in that client's particular format.

14. Engage in a rich dialogue with the leaders in your consulting firm on the firm's core competencies. Why are we so good at what we do? Why do we criticize common practices of our clients? Why are our standard procedures selected?

15. Create a packet (electronic or otherwise) of information about the firm, including phone numbers, email addresses, blank stationery (so you can write thank-you letters to clients), blank evaluation forms, the back-door number to your office voice mail . . . stuff like that.

16. Make travel easier by entering speed-dial numbers for airlines, hotels, and rental car companies. When everybody else on the plane is yelling at flight attendants, you can be calling the help desk and arranging changes in your flight, car, and hotel.

*17. **Know how to make your computer work with client projectors.*** Usually it's just an easy combination of keys, such as "Shift-F7" or a similar combination, but failure to know these keystrokes can cause an enormous amount of frustration and potential embarrassment at a client site.

*18. **Have examples of client reports. Give clients a vision of what you can provide for them if they are diligent and persistent.*** "If you do X, then you will achieve Y." Many adults are visual learners, and we need to provide visual examples of their future.

*19. **Find the real client.*** I have been burned more than once by following the directions of the person who engaged us, only to find out that the real clients were the people in the room—people who were totally alienated from the person who engaged us. I thought I was doing a great job, and I did do a wonderful job—of meeting all the needs of people who were not in the room. I learned that I had to check regularly for understanding by asking questions such as, "Is this what we need right now?" "These are my understandings about this group—are my assumptions accurate?" "What do we need to be doing right now to make the next 30 minutes valuable for you?"

*20. **Invest in ear candy.*** For you, this might range from James Taylor to Bruce Springsteen to Shawn Colvin to Johann Sebastian Bach to Billy Joel to Barenaked Ladies to Felix Mendelssohn to Devo to Aretha Franklin to Wolfgang Amadeus Mozart. There is too much noise in the world, created not so much by crying babies, howling animals, or screeching machinery as by whining adults. Put your iPod on "Shuffle" and let your CD collection move in mysterious ways, drowning out the world around you. Shut out the distractions of angry conversations with your Bose headphones or, if you are traveling light, with Sony noise-canceling earplugs, and immerse yourself in the "Goldberg Variations," followed by "Sweet Baby James," then the Mozart "Requiem" for a long flight; then, just as you are landing, crank it up to hear "R-E-S-P-E-C-T." However talkative your seatmate may be, he is unlikely to hold a candle to the conversations you will create with the musicians who sing and play for you in your private concert.

APPENDIX A

Needs Analysis

FORM A-1 **Overview**

To best meet your needs, we must first invest some of our time in learning more about you. This needs analysis gives us the information we have to have to make a proposal to you. It includes general background information as well as information about your goals and objectives. Based on your responses to the needs analysis, we will prepare a detailed proposal for your consideration. There is no cost for our preliminary analysis and proposal.

P A R T   I   **Contact Information**

Company name: _____

Address: _____

_____

_____

Telephone number: _____

Today's date: _____

Name of person completing form: _____

	Name	Phone/Fax	Address and Email
Chairman of the Board			
Administrative assistant to the Chairman of the Board			
CEO/President			
Administrative assistant to the CEO/President			
COO			
Administrative assistant to the COO			
CFO			
Administrative assistant to the CFO			
Managers			
Other key leadership team members			

P A R T   I I   Document Requests

It is very helpful for us to have copies of the following documents. Please send copies that can be maintained in our files.

Document	Available? (Yes/No)	Date Sent to Center	Date Received by Consultant
1. Annual reports (last 5 years)			
2. Strategic plan (or other goal-planning document in use)			
3. Marketing materials			
4. Technology plan (please include a description of Internet capabilities and technology applications in the classroom)			
5. Needs assessment, surveys, or other internal documents used within the past 12 months to assess system needs			

P A R T   I I I   Past Experiences

1. Please describe your most successful engagement with an outside consultant.

2. How did you measure success?

A. What were your goals and how were they established?

B. Can you break down what you mean by *success:* company-wide, by department, by division, etc.?

3. Please describe your most unsuccessful engagement with an outside consultant.

A. What did you consider your biggest challenge in not meeting success with this consultant?

B. What could this consultant have done differently that might have led to greater success?

| P A R T   I V | **Leadership Reflections on Critical Needs** |

Please identify the critical needs from the perspectives of the executive team. Please feel free to extend this response on additional paper.

Perspective	Critical Needs
Chairman of the Board	
Board CEO/President	
COO	
CFO	
Other key leadership team members	

P A R T V	Expectations

Based on what you presently know, what are your expectations for how we can best serve you?

Focus Area	Expectations
Other critical areas (please list)	

Thank you very much for taking the time to help us learn more about you. Please return this form and the requested information and we will prepare a detailed proposal for your consideration.

Organizational Forms

FORM B-1 **Pre-Engagement Conference**

Consultant's name: _____

Date of pre-engagement conference: _____

Client contact name and telephone number: _____

The purpose of this conference is to complete and clarify the needs analysis, identify specific expectations for a particular on-site engagement, and identify the people and groups within the client organization that will be part of the decisionmaking process.

P A R T I	Review of Needs Analysis

1. All questions in the needs analysis complete?   ❏ Yes   ❏ No

    Remarks:

2. All documents requested in the needs analysis received?   ❏ Yes   ❏ No

    Remarks:

3. Any additional elaboration by the client, particularly on client strengths and challenges:

P A R T I I	Client Expectations

1. Date of on-site engagement:

---

2. Objective of the engagement in the client's words:

---

3. Agenda, including specific arrival and departure times:

---

4. Is the consultant making a presentation to the client? If so:

   A. Presentation title:

   B. Presentation format (workshop, seminar, lecture, etc.):

   C. Setting (tables and chairs, auditorium, etc.):

   D. Audiovisual needs:

   E. Technology support needs:

   F. Participant materials provided by consultant:

   G. Participant materials provided by client:

   H. Participant names, titles, and contact information:

P A R T   I I I   Critical Client Decisionmaking Groups and People

1. Who will sign the final contract?

2. Who will approve the criteria for work?

3. Who will create specifications for work?

4. Who will approve change orders?

5. Who will evaluate the work at the conclusion of the engagement?

   Ask the client to complete this sentence: This day will be a success if . . . .

P A R T   I V   Travel Information

As you know, travel has become a lot more challenging recently, so I'd like to check on some of the logistical details with you.

1. Where is the closest airport to the presentation location?

2. How long does it take to drive to the airport from the presentation location?

3. Because I am required to check in at the airport two hours before departure, and my flight will depart at about _____ , it looks as if I'll need to leave the presentation location at _____ . Will that work with the agenda you are planning? Do we need to consider starting earlier in the morning?

4. As you have probably heard, flight schedules change frequently, sometimes daily. In case there is a last-minute change in the flight schedule, please give me your emergency contact number, including home phone and cell phone:

FORM B-2 **Client Engagement Checklist**

Consultant's name: _____

Initial customer contact/inquiry: _____

Client engagement checklist:

- ❏ Client name (state, city, organization acronym)
- ❏ Contact name, phone and fax numbers, email address
- ❏ Mailing address (if PO Box, street address as well)
- ❏ Date of engagement
- ❏ Speaking times
- ❏ Objectives for the presentation—"As a result of this engagement, what do you want to achieve?"
- ❏ Location of presentation
- ❏ Characteristics of place of presentation (auditorium, meeting room?)
- ❏ Audience—size, composition
- ❏ Audio/visual needs
- ❏ Assess type of workshop/presentation
- ❏ Status of inquiry—pending file and (?) on calendar until verbal confirmation
- ❏ Checklist on database in pending file under "Clients" until confirmed
- ❏ Schedule checked, fees discussed, presenter established
- ❏ Verify with presenter, confirm with client
- ❏ Enter onto calendar
    - ❏ Consultant initials—location
      [Example: DR-CA, Riverside]
    - ❏ Notes—contact name and phone number
- ❏ Enter into "Contacts"
    - ❏ Client information
    - ❏ Categories: New Contact, Client
    - ❏ Notes:
        - ❏ Notes from conversations, with date and initials of person entering
        - ❏ Date, consultant initials, and titles of presentations
        - ❏ Pre-engagement conference checklist from consultant
- ❏ Email checklist to Client Relations

FORM B-3   Client Engagement—
Confirmed Client into System

- ❑ Receive client engagement checklist
- ❑ Enter into Outlook
    - ❑ Calendar
        - ❑ Times of meeting/presentation/workshop
        - ❑ Title of presentation
        - ❑ Insert checklist into notes
    - ❑ Contacts—Insert checklist into notes
- ❑ Email checklist to consultant
- ❑ Set up file: paper and computer
    - ❑ Client folder in database
        - ❑ Clients
        - ❑ State
        - ❑ Client name (client named by state and city or district name)
    - ❑ Physical files (two)
        - ❑ Client file
        - ❑ Travel file
- ❑ Job tracking matrix
    - ❑ Entry by date of engagement
    - ❑ Contact name and phone number
    - ❑ Fee amount
    - ❑ Consultant rate
    - ❑ Client fee
    - ❑ Consultant agreement sent
    - ❑ Letter of agreement sent

FORM B-4 # Client Engagement—Letter of Agreement/Speaking Agreement

Letter of agreement

- ❑ Copies made—two originals, two copies
- ❑ Two originals to client with
    - ❑ W-9
    - ❑ Return envelope
    - ❑ Consultant information
    - ❑ Travel checklist
- ❑ Email letter of agreement to Finance
- ❑ Client file: original checklist and letter of agreement
- ❑ Check off on Job Tracking Matrix: "Letter of agreement sent"
- ❑ Letter of agreement returned; check off on Job Tracking Matrix

Speaking agreement, if applicable

- ❑ Enter onto speaking agreement
    - ❑ Client
    - ❑ Contact and phone number
    - ❑ Speaking fee
    - ❑ Date, times, and locations
    - ❑ Notes from previous client conversations
- ❑ Check off on Job Tracking Matrix
- ❑ Agreement returned; check off on Job Tracking Matrix

Consultant arrangements

- ❑ Set up phone conference with client
- ❑ Consultant completes phone conference, identifies handouts, if any
- ❑ Consultant makes travel arrangements

Form B-5 **Travel File Checklist**

When traveling, the following information should be with you. Your travel will be easier and stress minimized if the following details have been taken care of and are in a file where you know everything you need is in one place.

1. Airport information

   ❑ Nearest airport _____

   ❑ Distance from airport to presentation location _____

2. Hotel reservations

   ❑ Recommendation from client, if needed _____

   ❑ Always king bed/nonsmoking (or individual preference) _____

   ❑ Guaranteed late arrival _____

   ❑ Confirmation # _____

   ❑ Hotel reward # _____

   ❑ Hotel address _____

   _____

   ❑ Hotel phone number _____

Ask distance from airport and obtain directions from airport to hotel (from Yahoo or MapQuest or ask hotel staff if they have a map they can fax). Verify ground transportion arrangements: shuttle service, car service information, etc.

3. Where and when presenting

   ❑ Time to arrive _____

   ❑ Agenda of the day _____

   _____

   ❑ Address and directions to presentation from hotel _____

   _____

   _____

   ❑ Exact room/location within building where presenting _____

   _____

   _____

4. Presentation

   ❑ LCD viewer _____

   ❑ Podium if desired _____

   ❑ Request lapel (lavaliere) microphone _____

   ❑ Roundtable format for small groups (or individual preference) _____

   ❑ Large screen _____

5. Client information

   ❑ Copy of checklist with notes and phone numbers (cell and/or home) _____

   _____

   _____

   ❑ Relevant reference materials _____

   _____

   _____

   _____

6. Tools required for follow-up to presentation

   ❑ Envelope to hold business cards collected for personal follow-up

   _____

   ❑ Blank thank-you notes to write to key people directly following presentation

   _____

   _____

   _____

   _____

   _____

   _____

   _____

   _____

   _____

FORM B-6 **Follow-up Procedures**

1. Thank you note

2. Needs analysis

3. Evaluations

4. Feedback from consultant

5. Client questionnaire

6. Tracking

FORM B-7 **Client Engagement—Finance**

1. Enter client information into accounting software from information on checklist and letter of agreement

   _____

   _____

2. Establish invoicing dates for speaking fees and expenses _____

   _____

3. Invoice #1: Speaking fees and advance travel—45 days prior
   to engagement or upon receipt of letter of agreement   _____

4. Consultant expense reimbursements

   A. All receipts for engagement submitted to client for reimbursement   _____

   B. Items typically not reimbursable or billable to client:

      a. Liquor   _____

      b. Videos   _____

      c. First-class upgrades   _____

   TOTAL   _____

5. Invoice #2: Travel expenses invoice—Issued within two weeks
   following engagement

   A. Air fare—coach   _____

   B. Entered when passenger receipts received from travel agency   _____

   C. Consultant reviews itinerary and splits between applicable jobs

   D. Hotel—from consultant expense sheet   _____

   E. Meals—from consultant expense sheet   _____

   F. Parking, rental car, mileage   _____

   G. Any unpaid fees from Invoice #1   _____

   H. Subtract advance estimated travel if paid from Invoice #1   _____

   TOTAL   _____

Linking Your Time
with Your Mission

FORM C-1 **Time Log**

Instructions: Maintain a detailed log of time for two weeks. Use categories that are appropriate for you. Examples of categories to enter in the columns include: Planning, Email and Voice-Mail Responses, Exercise, Professional Reading, Counseling Direct Reports, Staff Meetings, Travel, Community Service, and Family.

Date: _____

[Enter your categories for each column; examples shown]

From (start time)	To (end time)	Total time (fraction of 1 hour)	Planning	Email	Voice-Mail Responses	Exercise	Professional Reading

Total: _____

Today's total hours: _____

After collecting at least 14 of these daily records, construct a pie chart that reflects your actual time allocation. Compare it to your priorities and evaluate whether changes are appropriate in the way you allocate your most important resource: your time.

1. What is your most important challenge right now?

2. What did you do today to make progress on your most important challenge?

Other questions that address your central challenges:

FORM C-2 **Master Task List**

Instructions: Use this form to start your time management system. Using as many pages as you need, list every single task that is now pending for you. Because you are using a single, comprehensive system, list all tasks, including those related to family obligations, professional requirements, community service, and other tasks from any list that you keep. The start of your journey to effective time management is the use of a single list for all tasks.

Prioritize each task using these codes:

A = Must be done by you and only you

B = Should be done by you, but will give way to A-level tasks

C = Request to be done by you, but can be delayed or delegated to others

Name: _____ Date: _____

Page _____ of _____ pages

Task	Priority (A, B, C)	Date of Origination

FORM C-3 **Daily Prioritized Task List**

Note: Create a new Daily Prioritized Task List every day. Throughout the day, add any new requests for your time. If you have more than six A priorities for today, you must either defer some of the A-level tasks or change some of those tasks to B-level priority.

Name: _____ Date: _____

Page _____ of _____ pages

Task	Priority (A, B, C)	Date of Origination

Form C-4 Project Task List

Instructions: Projects must be broken down into manageable tasks. Any task that takes more than the time allowed for a single uninterrupted work session must be broken down into several different tasks. In general, if a task takes more than three hours to complete, it is not a task, but a project.

Project Name: _____ Start Date: _____

Task	Person Responsible	Start Date	Deadline

Journaling

FORM D-1 **Reflective Journal**

Keep a journal with the most important questions that force you to address your key challenges. After you have accumulated entries for several weeks, discuss them with a mentor, coach, colleague, or other trusted person.

Date: _____

1. What did you learn today?

   A. About a client?

   B. About a colleague?

   C. About yourself?

2. What difficult issue did you confront today?

_____

A. With a client?

_____

B. With a colleague?

_____

C. With yourself?

_____

References

Benson, H., & Klipper, M. Z. (1975). *The relaxation response.* New York: HarperTorch.

Benson, H., & Proctor, W. (2003). *The breakout principle: How to activate the natural trigger that maximizes creativity, athletic performance, productivity and personal well-being.* New York: Scribner.

Block, P., & 30 flawless consultants, assisted by Markowitz, A. M. (2001). *The flawless consulting fieldbook & companion: A guide to understanding your expertise.* San Francisco: Jossey-Bass/Pfeiffer.

Buckingham, M., & Clifton, D. O. (2001). *Now, discover your strengths.* New York: Free Press.

Buckingham, M., & Coffman, C. (1999). *First, break all the rules: What the world's greatest managers do differently.* New York: Simon & Schuster.

Cameron, K. S., & Caza, A. (2004, February). Contributions to positive organizational scholarship. *American Behavioral Scientist, 47*(6).

Caruso, D. R., & Salovey, P. (2004). *The emotionally intelligent manager: How to develop and use the four key emotional skills of leadership.* San Francisco: Jossey-Bass.

Christensen, C. M. (2003). *The innovator's dilemma.* New York: HarperBusiness.

Collins, J. (2001). *Good to great: Why some companies make the leap . . . and others don't.* New York: HarperCollins.

Covey, S. R. (1989). *The 7 habits of highly effective people: Powerful lessons in personal change.* New York: Fireside Books.

Einhorn, C. S. (2004, October 10). A manager falls hard, but sticks to the path. *New York Times,* p. 25.

Enron Corporation. (2000). *1999 Annual Report.* Houston, TX: Author.

Friedman, M., & Friedman, R. (1980). *Free to choose: A personal statement.* Orlando, FL: Harcourt.

Froggatt, C. C. (2001). *Work naked: Eight essential principles for peak performance in the virtual workplace.* San Francisco: Jossey-Bass.

Fromm, E. (1976; 1979 ed.). *To have or to be.* London: Abacus.

Galbraith, J. K. Retrieved March 22, 2005 from http://www.brainyquote.com/quotes/quotes/j/johnkennet150393.html

Gerber, M. E. (2001). *The e-myth revisited: Why most small businesses don't work and what to do about it* (2d ed.). New York: HarperBusiness.

Goleman, D. (1998). *Working with emotional intelligence.* New York: Bantam Books.

Goleman, D., Boyatzis, R., & McKee, A. (2002). *Primal leadership: Realizing the power of emotional intelligence.* Boston: Harvard Business School Press.

Kanter, R. M. (2004). *Confidence: How winning streaks and losing streaks begin and end.* New York: Crown Business.

Kaufman, Charlie (Writer/Producer), & Gondry, M. (Writer/Director). (2004). *Eternal sunshine of the spotless mind* [Motion picture]. United States: Focus Features.

Khalsa, M. (1999). *Let's get real or let's not play: The demise of 20th century selling and the advent of helping clients succeed.* Salt Lake City, UT: Franklin Covey.

Kim, W. C., & Mauborgne, R. (2004, October). Blue ocean strategy. *Harvard Business Review, 82*(10), 76–84.

Koshiyama, M. (2003). *Journal 10+, 2003–2013 ed.* Because Time Flies, Inc.

Kotter, J. P. (1996). *Leading change.* Boston: Harvard Business School Press.

McCormick, M. H. (1984). *What they don't teach you at Harvard Business School: Notes from a street-smart executive.* New York: Bantam Books.

Mitchell, B. (1994). *Bet on cowboys, not horses.* Shaker Heights, OH: York Publishing.

Oliver, S. (1993, August 16). Slouches make better operators: Aspen Tree Software designs personnel questionnaires and productivity measurement software. *Forbes,* p. 104.

Olson, M. A. (2002). *Moving beyond church growth: An alternative vision for congregations.* Minneapolis, MN: Fortress Publishers.

Olson, M. A. (1992). *The evangelical pastor: Pastoral leadership for a witnessing people.* Minneapolis, MN: Augsburg Fortress.

Peters, T. J., & Austin, N. (1989). *A passion for excellence: The leadership difference.* New York: Warner Books.

Peters, T. J., & Waterman, Jr., R. H. (1982). *In search of excellence: Lessons from America's best-run companies.* New York: Warner Books.

Raisel, E. M. (1999). *The McKinsey way: Using the techniques of the world's top strategic consultants to help you and your business.* New York: McGraw-Hill.

Reeves, D. B. (2004). *Assessing educational leaders: Evaluating performance for improved individual and organizational results.* Thousand Oaks, CA: Corwin Press.

Reeves, D. B. (2002a). *The daily disciplines of leadership: How to improve student achievement, staff motivation, and personal organization* (1st ed.). [The Jossey-Bass education series.] San Francisco: Jossey-Bass.

Reeves, D. B. (2002b). *The leader's guide to standards: A blueprint for educational equity and excellence.* San Francisco: Jossey-Bass.

Rigby, D. K., & Ledingham, D. (2004, November 1). CRM done right. *Harvard Business Review, 82*(11), 118–129.

Schwartz, F. N. (1989, January-February). Management women and the new facts of life. *Harvard Business Review, 67*(1), 65–76.

Seligman, M. (1998). *Learned optimism: How to change your mind and your life.* New York: Pocket Books.

Smith, H. W. (1994). *The 10 natural laws of successful time and life management: Proven strategies for increased productivity and inner peace.* New York: Warner Books.

Stewart, T. (2003, January). Motivating people [Special issue]. *Harvard Business Review, 81*(1).

Sutton, R. (2004, February). The HBR list of breakthrough ideas for 2004. *Harvard Business Revew, 82*(2), 13–37.

Index

The Center for Performance Assessment is an international consulting organization dedicated to providing extraordinary performance through extraordinary learning. The Center works with businesses, nonprofit organizations, governmental entities, and school systems throughout the world. To learn more about how the Center can help your organization achieve extraordinary results, contact the CEO, Dr. Douglas Reeves, at (800) 844-6599, ext. 512, or on the Web at www.LeadAndLearn.com.

**CENTER FOR
PERFORMANCE
ASSESSMENT**

317 Inverness Way South, Suite 150 ▪ Englewood, CO 80112
(800) 844-6599 or (303) 504-9312 ▪ Fax (303) 504-9417